25 WAYS
TO WIN
WITH
PEOPLE

HOW TO MAKE OTHERS FEEL LIKE A MILLION BUCKS

JOHN C.
MAXWELL

AND LES PAR

NELSON BUSINESS
A Division of Thomas Nelson Publishers
Since 1798

www.thomasnelson.com

Published in Nashville, Tennessee, by Thomas Nelson, Inc.

Unless otherwise noted, Scripture quotations are taken from the NEW AMERICAN STANDARD BIBLE®, © Copyright The Lockman Foundation 1960, 1962, 1963, 1968, 1971, 1972, 1973, 1975, 1977. Used by permission.

Nelson Books titles may be purchased in bulk for educational, business, fundraising, or sales promotional use. For information, please e-mail SpecialMarkets @ThomasNelson.com.

Published in association with Yates & Yates, LLP, Attorneys and Counselors, Orange, California.

Library of Congress Cataloging-in-Publication Data

Maxwell, John C., 1947-
    25 ways to win with people : how to make others feel like a million bucks
/ John C. Maxwell and Les Parrott.
        p. cm.
Includes bibliographical references.
    ISBN 978-0-7852-6094-3 (hardcover)
    ISBN 978-0-7852-7954-9 (international)
    1. Interpersonal relations—Religious aspects—Christianity. 2.
Interpersonal communication—Religious aspects—Christianity. 3.
Interpersonal relations. 4. Interpersonal communication. I. Title: Twenty-five ways to win with people. II. Parrott, Les. III. Title.
    BV4597.52.M393 2005
    158.2—dc22

                                                                        2005000103

Printed in the United States of America

13 14 15 QG 16 15 14 13 12

To Tom Mullins,

You are like the Pied Piper. When you walk into a room, people instantly want to follow you. More than anyone I know, you embody the 25 ways to win with people. You make everyone around you feel like a million bucks—including me!

—JOHN C. MAXWELL

To Mike Ingram and Monty Ortman,

Few people build a better business team, win more respect, and achieve bigger results than you two. You both have a winsome way of relating to everyone you meet. Your generous spirits and your investment in people will pay dividends for decades. I'm a better person for having known you both.

—LES PARROTT

CONTENTS

❧

❧

CONTENTS

ACKNOWLEDGMENT

Thank you to Charlie Wetzel
for his help in writing this book.

LIFE'S GREATEST JOY
BY JOHN C. MAXWELL

In the spring of 2004, soon after turning in the finished manuscript of *Winning with People*, the publisher sent out a number of advance copies of the book, as they often do, to get feedback and endorsements. One of the people who received a copy was Les Parrott.

Now, you may know Dr. Les Parrott from any one of a number of his successes: he is a professor of psychology at Seattle Pacific University, the founder of the Center for Relationship Development, a nationally successful speaker to Fortune 500 companies, and a best-selling author of books such as *High-Maintenance Relationships* and *Love the Life You Live*. He has been a guest on CNN, *The NBC Nightly News*, *Oprah*, and other programs. But I know Les as a friend. In fact, when I first met Les, he was only a kid. He was just beginning his Ph.D. studies in psychology. And the instant I met him, I could see he was sharp. I knew he would soon be a rising star.

In the summer of 2004, I got a phone call from Les. "John," he said, "I loved *Winning with People*. I think it's going to help a lot of folks. It's going to prompt them to change their attitudes and see their relationships with people in a whole new light. And by the way, I wrote a nice endorsement for it. But I have an idea for you. I think you should write a sequel."

I had put my whole heart and a lifetime of relational learning into *Winning with People*, so I was a bit skeptical. But I have a lot of respect for Les, and he always has great ideas, so I was all ears.

"What's your idea?" I asked.

"I've watched you with people for years," Les continued. "When you spend time with people, you make them feel like a million bucks. You've made *me* feel like a million bucks. I bet you could sit down and come up with a couple of dozen specific things that you've mastered that you could teach others to do." That got my juices flowing. "And John, I think you should call the book *How to Make Others Feel Like a Million Bucks*."

Then Les started to rattle off some of the things he thought I should teach, such as giving others a reputation to uphold, mining the gold of good intentions, telling good stories, and helping people win. The more I thought, the more I liked the idea. *Winning with People* had been written to change the fundamental way people approached relationships. Doing what it suggests would take a period of time to accomplish. On the other hand, the book Les was suggesting would be able to help people learn specific skills that could be mastered in a matter of days.

"You know," I said after a long pause, "it's a great idea. Why don't you write it with me?"

Les was surprised.

"I think we'd make a great team," I told him. "You said yourself that you've watched me for years. You're a trained psychologist. Together we'll figure out what skills to write about. I'll teach how I work with people, and you can help people understand the psychology behind the practices."

And that's how *25 Ways to Win with People* came to be written. Les and I had a great time comparing notes, talking about relationships, and telling stories. My one reservation is that Les insisted on telling so many stories about me. I'm not anywhere near as good as Les makes me out to be. Like everyone, I've done stupid things, stepped on toes, and hurt people's feelings. But I've always tried to do my best. And I'm still working daily to improve my skills with others.

And I can tell you this: these skills really do work! Les and I believe that if you practice the skills in this book, your life will change. Why? Because will be able to help others see themselves in a positive light. You will often make them feel like a million bucks.

I believe there is no greater joy in life than seeing others blossom, grow, and reach their potential. This book can help you have a part in making that happen for the people in your life.

BETTER FOR HAVING KNOWN YOU

BY LES PARROTT

Some people possess an invisible quality that draws others to them like a magnet. They're more than just likable. Their charisma defines everything they do and every encounter they have. Accordingly they build better teams, win more respect, and achieve bigger results. Are they merely lucky in life, blessed with personality traits that spell success without effort? Not on your life!

This alluring and invisible trait is not inherited as much as it is honed. It's a captivating spirit that can be taught and caught. For too long people haven't tried to cultivate these qualities because of the false impression that you either have "it" or you don't. This book will help change that misinformed notion. For here you will find twenty-five of the most compelling keys to unlocking a charismatic spirit—a spirit that will help you win with almost everyone you encounter.

WHY WE'RE WRITING THIS BOOK TOGETHER

No one who has ever come in close contact with John Maxwell has walked away unaffected. That's certainly true for me. As a mentor, John has left a permanent imprint on nearly every aspect of my personal and professional life. More than twenty years ago, before I launched into my graduate training to become a clinical psychologist, I flew from my home in Chicago to spend a week with John in San Diego for the sole purpose of soaking up his wisdom. Some years later, it was John who encouraged me to write books and begin a speaking career. And these days, a dozen books later, when we happen to share the same platform, John is always my biggest fan. It's no exaggeration to say that John believes in me more than I could ever have the right to ask.

I'm a better person because John Maxwell is in my life. John taught me how to summon my courage; how to find my purpose and tap into my passion; how to hone my vision and strive toward my goals. He taught me how to "fail forward," how to make each day count, and how to cultivate a can-do attitude. Interaction with a people person like John can have that kind of an impact on you. Directly and indirectly, John has taught me multiple and invaluable life lessons. But more than anything, John has taught me how to win with people. He has a winsome way of relating to nearly everyone— whether it's a server at a restaurant or the chairman of a major corporation.

THE SECRETS OF INTERPERSONAL MAGIC

Down through the decades, I've studied John as he lifts people up. And as a friend, I wanted to know how I could personally cultivate more of his interpersonal magic. Anyone who has spent even a short period of time with John knows that he puts you at ease and makes you feel good. Not the kind of "good" that comes from a flippant compliment or insincere affirmation—and certainly not from a smarmy or manipulative slap on the back. I'm talking about the kind of goodness that comes from knowing he genuinely wants the best for you. He's pulling for you and wants you to win.

I've kept my eyes focused on even the most minute of interactions. Time and again, John displays an almost uncanny ability to disarm, entertain, and engage whomever he meets. In other words, he has the ability to make others feel like a million bucks. So as he already told you, one day I approached him with the idea of his sharing the secrets of his magnetic personality to help you learn to do what he does. When John invited me to write this book with him, I spent hours with him to draw out the things he does reflexively on a daily basis. And I also talked extensively to John's friends and staff. I heard story after story about the ways John has won with them and added value to their lives. I tell many of these stories in the book so that you can "see" the practices in action.

WITHIN YOUR REACH

The twenty-five secrets we include in this book have the potential to change your life. They can help you to become the kind of magnetic person who lights up the room when you arrive. These skills are readily learnable. They are not just for a lucky few who seem to be hardwired with exclusive qualities. They are within reach of anyone who wants them. And they are crucial for anyone wanting to win with people.

1

START WITH
YOURSELF

Your relationships can only be as healthy as you are.
—Neil Clark Warren

LES . . . ON STARTING WITH YOURSELF

If you want to win with people, you've got to be a winner
yourself—or at the very least be on your way to becoming
one. There's no avoiding this simple fact.

As a psychologist specializing in relationships, I've seen
hundreds of people in therapy. I've spoken to hundreds of
thousands in seminars. I've written more than a dozen books
on the subject. People close to me understand that I'm pas-
sionate about helping others win with people. But if there is
one thing I know, it's that a new tip or technique to win with
others will fall flat if you don't start with yourself.

Let me say it straight. If you try to practice the "ways" of winning with people that you are about to learn in the following chapters before you give serious attention to how you can be a winner yourself, you'll be sorely disappointed. However, if you will first take the time to focus on yourself, you'll soon be ready to focus on others.

You've Got to Start with Yourself

William James, the first American psychologist, said, "The hell to be endured hereafter, of which theology tells, is no worse than the hell we make for ourselves in this world by habitually fashioning our characters in the wrong way." If we do not form a winning character, we are sure to lose with other people. That's why this first step is so significant. In fact, there are at least two compelling reasons why winning with people hinges on starting with yourself.

You Can't Be Happy Without Being Healthy

Psychology used to think it was critical to focus on—and then eliminate—negative emotions. We now know there is a better way. A new generation of research has shifted psychology's primary analysis from that of misery to an understanding of wellness.

The new research reveals that you can't be happy simply by being unencumbered by depression, stress, or anxiety. No—you can't be happy unless you are healthy. And there's a lot more to health than not being sick. Emotional health is more than the absence of dysfunctional emotions. Emotional health is at the center of winning with people.

You Can't Give What You Don't Have

One of the oldest psychological truisms in the world is that you cannot give what you do not have. In fact, like every other psychologist-in-training, when I first began my graduate education, I was urged to get into psychotherapy myself. "Les," my advisor said, "as a psychologist, you will only be able to take a person as far as you have gone yourself." Why? Because you cannot give what you do not have. You cannot enjoy others until you enjoy yourself.

Harry Firestone said, "You get the best out of others when you give the best of yourself." So true. But if the best you have isn't any better than what those "others" already possess, you'll never take them any higher than they already are.

The bottom line? If you are not becoming a winner, you'll find it almost impossible to win with others. But here's the good news: your desire and attempts to win with others help to make you a winner. It's what American essayist Charles Warner was getting at when he said, "No one can sincerely try to help another without helping himself."

How to Be a Winner

"There's a period of life when we swallow a knowledge of ourselves," said Pearl Bailey, "and it becomes either good or sour inside." Everyone has little anxieties and insecurities. If I were to ask you to describe a winning person, a person who is whole and healthy, you might say something about this person being confident, warm, kind, stable, giving, and so on. And you'd be right, in a sense. But there's more to becoming a winner than having a list of enviable attributes. Being a winner comes down to one thing: your value.

Winners are valuable. Ask any star athlete or gold medalist who has just signed a multimillion-dollar endorsement deal. But truth be told, being a winner, in the purest sense of the word, has nothing to do with your performance, your salary, or your earning potential. It has to do with your value and whether or not you have *owned* it. When you embrace your own personal value, when you are secure in who you are, then you have become a winner.

Here are a few ways of doing just that:

∞ RECOGNIZE YOUR VALUE. On more than one occasion, I've told the story of being on a speaking platform with my friend Gary Smalley when he did something that captivated the crowd. Before an audience of nearly ten thousand people, Gary held out a crisp fifty-dollar bill and asked them, "Who would like this fifty-dollar bill?" Hands started going up everywhere.

"I am going to give this fifty dollars to one of you," he said, "but first let me do this." He proceeded to crumple up the bill. Then he asked, "Who still wants it?" The same hands went up in the air.

"Well," he continued, "what if I do this?" He dropped it on the ground and started to grind it into the floor with his shoe. He picked it up, all crumpled and dirty. "Now, who still wants it?" Again, hands went into the air.

"You have all learned a valuable lesson," Gary said. "No matter what I do to the money, you still want it because it doesn't decrease in value. It is still worth fifty dollars."

Gary's simple illustration underscores a profound point. Many times in our lives we are dropped, crumpled, and ground into the dirt by the decisions we make or the circumstances that come our way. We may feel as though we are worthless, insignificant in our own eyes and in the eyes of others. But no matter what has happened or what will happen, we *never* lose our value as human beings. Nothing can take that away. Never forget that.

❧ ACCEPT YOUR VALUE. How many times have you heard people say, "He has issues"? What they mean is that the person is stuck. The person is not healthy. He's got a hang-up. He's uncomfortable in his own skin. It's what we psychologists are getting at when we talk about self-acceptance.

Let's face it. All of us walking around on this planet have insecurities and issues that we wish we could change about ourselves. But certain things we can't. Some things about us just *are*. Maybe you weren't born with the kind of looks you would like. Or you aren't as tall as you desire. Your genes dealt you a hand that you've eventually got to accept—either that or you reject your personal value and spend your days trying to compensate for your insecurities. You become hung up, stuck on not being dealt a better hand.

The term *acceptance* comes from the Latin *ad capere* that means "to take to oneself." In other words, inherent in the process of accepting others is the act of self-acceptance. I'll say it again: you will never win with people until *you* become a winner.

❧ INCREASE YOUR VALUE. Perhaps you already recognize and accept your value. Maybe you know at the center of your being, deep in your soul, that you are loved by God and are of inestimable value. Congratulations! The next step is to increase your value to others by solving as many of your problems as you can. In other words, you need to maximize who you are by overcoming or fixing those things that are within your power to change.

You may struggle with a hair-trigger temper, for example. Maybe you have difficulty setting boundaries or taking responsibility. Maybe you have some bad habits, or perhaps your attitude needs an overhaul. All of us have hurdles we can overcome. Forty-five percent of Americans report that they would change a bad habit if they could.[1] The truth is, they can change. Each of us can improve ourselves whenever we decide to.

In his book *Teaching the Elephant to Dance* (Crown, 1990), James Belasco described how trainers shackle young elephants with heavy chains to deeply embedded stakes. In that way the elephant learns to stay in its place. Older, more powerful elephants that have been trained in this way never try to leave—even though they have the strength to pull up the stake and walk away. Their conditioning limits their movements. Eventually, with only a small, unattached metal bracelet on their legs, they stand in place—even though the stakes are actually gone!

It's a story you've probably heard before, but like the powerful elephants, many people are bound by the restraints of previous conditioning. Just as the unattached chain around the elephant's leg keeps it from moving, some people impose needless limits on their personal progress. Don't let this happen to you. Don't mindlessly accept restraints on your abilities. Challenge them and keep growing.

∽ BELIEVE IN YOUR VALUE. Once you've recognized your value, accepted it, and increased it, you've eventually got to believe it. You've got to believe it with such conviction that you'd be willing to bank on it.

Chuck Wepner never learned this lesson. As a boxer, he earned the nickname "The Bayonne Bleeder" because of the punishment he took even while winning. In the boxing world he was what's called "a catcher," a fighter who often uses his head to block the other guy's punches. Wepner continually pressured his opponent until he either won or got knocked out. He never cared how many shots he had to absorb before landing a knockout blow. Trainer Al Braverman called him "the gutsiest fighter I ever met. He was in a league of his own. He didn't care about pain. If he got cut or elbowed, he never looked at me or the referee for help. He was a fighter in the purest sense of the word."

When Wepner knocked out Terry Henke in the eleventh round in Salt Lake City, boxing promoter Don King offered Wepner a title shot against then–heavyweight champion George Foreman. But when Ali defeated Foreman, Wepner found himself scheduled to fight "The Greatest"— Muhammad Ali. On the morning of the fight, Wepner gave his wife a pink negligee and told her she would "soon be sleeping with the heavyweight champion of the world."

Ali scored a technical knockout with just nineteen seconds remaining in the fight. But there was a moment—one glorious moment in the ninth round—when a hamlike paw to Ali's chest knocked the reigning champion off his feet.

Wepner recalled, "When Ali was down, I remember saying to my ringman, Al Braverman, 'Start the car, we're going to the bank, we're millionaires.' And Al said to me, 'You'd better turn around. Because he's getting up.'" After the fight,

Wepner's wife pulled the negligee out of her purse and asked, "Do I go to Ali's room or does he come to mine?" (see www.wepnerhomestead.com)

That story would be nothing more than an odd boxing footnote except for one thing. A struggling writer was watching the fight. And then it suddenly struck him: *There it is*, he said to himself. "So I went home and I started writing. And I wrote for three days straight." That's how writer and actor Sylvester Stallone described the birth of the Academy Award–winning movie *Rocky* to James Lipton on *Inside the Actor's Studio*.

The movie studio offered the struggling writer an unprecedented $400,000 for his script, but Stallone refused the money, choosing instead just $20,000 and the right to play the part of Rocky for actor's minimum wage, a paltry $340 a week. The studio also made an offer to Wepner since the movie was based on his life. He could receive a flat fee of $70,000 or 1 percent of the movie's gross profits. Wanting the guaranteed payday, Wepner took the $70,000, a decision that ultimately cost him $8 million. Today Chuck Wepner lives in Bayonne and works as a liquor salesman.

The same thing happens whenever you sell yourself short. If you don't believe that you have something of great value to offer another person—namely yourself—you'll never truly win with people. Who you are is the greatest asset you'll ever possess. And as long as you recognize this valuable asset, accept it, increase it, and believe it with deep conviction, the ways of winning with people in this book can become a part of your character. And when they come from the heart, they work like a charm.

JOHN ... WITH A MAXWELL MENTORING MOMENT

If I could meet you in person, one of the first things I would tell you is that I believe in you. You may find that hard to swallow because I don't even know you. But I do know this: everyone has value and something of value to offer others. One of my missions in life is to see that value in others, help them discover it, and encourage them to reach their potential. You can become a winner and help others do the same.

That's why I want to mentor you. I may not be able to sit down with you in person, but I've written this book with Les because I want to help you. In each chapter ahead, I will come alongside you for a mentoring moment and teach you a specific way to make others feel like a million bucks. It's my way of helping you win with people. And when we're done, I want to suggest that you seek out a face-to-face mentor, a winner who can add value to you and walk you through many of life's additional lessons.

LES ... ON BRINGING IT HOME

Each of the chapters in this book closes with a piece on bringing it home. It's designed to help you put the chapter's "winning way" into action. This little outline has served me well, so I pass it along to you.

To apply John's teaching to your own life . . .

Forget about:

Whatever makes you feel insecure.

Ask:

How can I increase my value in order to benefit others, rather than just myself?

Do it:

List the things you can improve about yourself (bad habits to break, etc.), along with specific steps to take to make the improvements.

Remember:

Your relationships can only be as healthy as you are.

2

PRACTICE THE
30-SECOND RULE

*He who waits to do a great deal of good at once,
will never do anything.*
—SAMUEL JOHNSON

LES ... ON SEEING THE PRACTICE IN ACTION

One of the most valuable lessons in winning with people that
I have ever learned from John is the 30-Second Rule: within
the first thirty seconds of a conversation, say something
encouraging to a person.

John is a master at it. While I was sitting in a meeting at
one of his companies a short time ago, John entered the room
and within just a few minutes said something encouraging to
each person around the table.

"David, I heard you hit it out of the park this morning on
that conference call."

"Larry, you are making me look so good with that consultation in Denver. Thank you."

"Kevin, I just saw the numbers for April. Nobody else in the world sees and seizes an opportunity the way you do."

"Les, I'm so glad you made the trip out here to be with us today. I know you're going to add tremendous value to our discussion."

Very early on, John had genuinely encouraged each one of us. And it seemed almost effortless. Since I was trying to learn more about John's winning ways with people, after the meeting I asked John to tell me about what he did. That's when I first heard the term "the 30-Second Rule."

"I learned this from my father," John said. "Years ago, he was the president of a college, and I would often walk across the campus with him. He continually stopped to say encouraging things to the students. When I was tempted to complain, I would look at the students' faces and realize Dad had deposited good words inside of them.

"People never forget that kind of encouragement," John continued. "Yesterday I talked to my dad on the phone, and he excitedly told me about his many former students who keep coming to Florida from all over the United States to see him. He was surprised that they would go out of their way to see him, but I wasn't. The 30-Second Rule that Dad had practiced with everyone every day was returning to him big time."

"I've seen you do this for years," I told John, "but I never knew it was something you picked up from your dad."

"I've learned a lot of great lessons from my dad. He's an incredible leader," John replied. "I practice this rule every day with everyone I meet. You see, someone once said to me, 'Be kind . . . everyone you meet is fighting a hard battle.' People everywhere need a good word, an uplifting compliment to fire their hopes and dreams. It takes very little effort to do, but it really lifts people up."

JOHN . . . WITH A MAXWELL MENTORING MOMENT

When most people meet others, they search for ways to make themselves look good. The key to the 30-Second Rule is reversing this practice. When you make contact with people, instead of focusing on yourself, search for ways to make *them* look good.

Every day before I meet with people, I pause to think about something encouraging I can tell them. What I say can be one of many things: I might thank them for something they've done for me or for a friend. I might tell others about one of their accomplishments. I might praise them for a personal quality they exhibit. Or I might simply compliment their appearance. The practice isn't complicated, but it does take some time, effort, and discipline. The reward for practicing it is huge, because it really makes a positive impact on people.

If you desire to encourage others by practicing the 30-Second Rule, then remember these things the next time you meet people:

THE 30-SECOND RULE GIVES PEOPLE THE TRIPLE-A TREATMENT

All people feel better and do better when you give them *attention*, *affirmation*, and *appreciation*. The next time you make contact with people, begin by giving them your undivided attention during the first thirty seconds. Affirm them and show your appreciation for them in some way. Then watch what happens. You will be surprised by how positively they respond. And if you have trouble remembering to keep your focus on them instead of on yourself, then perhaps the words of William King will help you. He said, "A gossip is one who talks to you about other people. A bore is one who talks to you about himself. And a brilliant conversationalist is one who talks to you about yourself."

> "A gossip is one who talks to you about other people. A bore is one who talks to you about himself. And a brilliant conversationalist is one who talks to you about yourself."
>
> —WILLIAM KING

THE 30-SECOND RULE GIVES PEOPLE ENERGY

Psychologist Henry H. Goddard conducted a study on energy levels in children using an instrument he called the "ergograph." His findings are fascinating. He discovered that when tired children were given a word of praise or commendation, the ergograph showed an immediate upward surge of energy in the children. When the children were criticized or discouraged, the ergograph showed that their physical energy took a sudden nosedive.

You may have already discovered this intuitively. When someone praises you, doesn't your energy level go up? And when you are criticized, doesn't that comment drag you down? Words have great power.

What kind of environment do you think you could create if you continually affirmed people when you first came into contact with them? Not only would you encourage them, but you would also become an energy carrier. Whenever you walked into a room, the people would light up! You would help to create the kind of environment everyone loves. Just your presence alone would brighten people's days.

THE 30-SECOND RULE INSTILLS MOTIVATION

Vince Lombardi, the famed Green Bay Packers football coach, was a feared disciplinarian. But he was also a great motivator. One day he chewed out a player who had missed several blocking assignments. After practice, Lombardi stormed into the locker room and saw that the player was sitting at his locker, head down, dejected. Lombardi mussed his hair, patted him on the shoulder, and said, "One of these days, you're going to be the best guard in the NFL."

That player was Jerry Kramer, and Kramer says he carried that positive image of himself for the rest of his career. "Lombardi's encouragement had a tremendous impact on my whole life," Kramer said. He went on to become a member of the Green Bay Packers Hall of Fame and a member of the NFL's All-50-Year Team.

Everybody needs motivation from time to time. Using the 30-Second Rule helps encourage people to be and do their best. Never underestimate the power of motivation:

- ◆ Motivation helps people who know what they should do . . . to do it!

- ◆ Motivation helps people who know what commitment they should make . . . to make it!
- ◆ Motivation helps people who know what habit they should break . . . to break it!
- ◆ Motivation helps people who know what path they should take . . . to take it!

Motivation makes it possible to accomplish what you should accomplish.

One of the great side benefits of the 30-Second Rule is that it also helps you. You can't help others without also helping yourself. Benjamin Franklin realized this truth, and he encouraged others with it. In a letter to John Paul Jones, Franklin wrote:

> Hereafter, if you should observe an occasion to give your officers and friends a little more praise than is their due, and confess more fault than you can justly be charged with, you will only become the sooner for it, a great captain. Criticizing and censuring almost everyone you have to do with, will diminish friends, increase enemies, and thereby hurt your affairs.

If you want others to feel good about themselves and to feel glad every time they see you, then practice the 30-Second Rule.

Those who add to us, draw us to them. Those who subtract, cause us to withdraw.

Remember this: those who add to us, draw us to them. Those who subtract, cause us to withdraw.

LES ... ON BRINGING IT HOME

Social psychologists have studied "first impressions" for decades. If you want to make an impression that is lasting and positive, we now know what works and what doesn't. And John's 30-Second Rule is one of the most effective means for finding success in this area. In research it's called the "primacy effect," and its initial impact goes a long way in making others feel connected with you.[1]

To apply John's teaching to your own life . . .

Forget about:

Searching for ways to make yourself look good.
Instead, search for ways to make others look good.

Ask:

What positive, encouraging thing can I say to each person I will see today?

Do it:

Give everyone you meet the Triple-A Treatment—attention, affirmation, and appreciation.

Remember:

Within the first thirty seconds of a conversation, say something encouraging.

3

LET PEOPLE KNOW YOU NEED THEM

*The greatest compliment that was ever paid me
was when someone asked me what I thought,
and attended to my answer.*
—HENRY DAVID THOREAU

LES ... ON SEEING THE PRACTICE IN ACTION

One day I asked John the secret to getting people to join a team, and he told me it could be found in a single sentence: "I can't do it without you." He went on to say that great leaders stumble when they believe people need *them* instead of recognizing that the very opposite is true. "Leaders can become great," said John, "only when they realize that *they* are the ones who need people."

As we talked, John pulled a laminated card from his desk drawer and told me he had developed a tool years ago for asking people for help. "Les, I wrote this back in 1974," he said. "I was facing a major building project and I needed to raise more than a million dollars. It was the first time I understood how far over my head I truly was in leadership.

"That's when I realized that if I was ever to achieve something great," John continued, "it would be the result of turning the dream from *me* to *we*." I scribbled down that phrase, intending to "borrow" it for an upcoming lecture. John went on, "I also realized that any dream I could achieve without the help of other people was too small."

Then John handed me the laminated card. On it were these words:

I Have a Dream

History tells us that in every age there comes a time when leaders must come forth to meet the needs of the hour. Therefore, there is no potential leader who does not have an opportunity to better mankind. Those around him also have the same privilege. Fortunately, I believe that God has surrounded me with those who will accept the challenge of this hour.

My dream allows me to . . .

- ◆ Give up at any moment all that I am in order to receive all that I can become.
- ◆ Sense the invisible so I can do the impossible.
- ◆ Trust God's resources since the dream is bigger than all my abilities and acquaintances.

- Continue when discouraged, for where there is no faith in the future, there is no power in the present.
- Attract winners, because big dreams draw big people.
- See my people and myself in the future. Our dream is the promise of what we shall one day be.

Yes, I have a dream. It is greater than any of my gifts. It is as large as the world, but it begins with one. Won't you join me?

—John Maxwell

"Les," he said, "I've given these cards out by the hundreds, and I have seen people time and again join up to help me accomplish my dream for one primary reason—because I let them know I needed them."

JOHN . . . WITH A MAXWELL MENTORING MOMENT

The day that I realized I could no longer do everything myself was a major step in my development as a person and a leader. I've always had vision, plenty of ideas, and vast amounts of energy. But when the vision gets bigger than you, you really only have two choices: give up on the vision or get help. I chose the latter.

When the vision gets bigger than you, you really only have two choices: give up on the vision or get help.

No matter how successful you are, no matter how important or accomplished, you *do* need people. That's why you need to let them know that you cannot win without them. President Woodrow Wilson said, "We should not only use all the brains we have—but all that we can borrow." Why stop with just their brains? Enlist people's hands and hearts, too! Another president, Lyndon Johnson, was right when he said, "There are no problems we cannot solve together, and very few that we can solve by ourselves."

Asking others for help is a great way to make them feel like a million bucks. Why?

PEOPLE NEED TO BE NEEDED

Have you ever stopped to ask someone for directions? You roll down your car window and ask a passerby, "Can you tell me how to find Larry's Market?" Nearly every time, people stop whatever they are doing and help if they can—even if it means crossing the street or standing in traffic. They may even repeat the directions a couple of times to make sure you get it. Why? Because whenever a person feels that he or she knows something you don't, it gives that person an ego boost. Everyone likes to be an expert, even if it's for a moment. It gives them a great sense of superiority and of accomplishment when they help. That translates into an increased sense of self-worth. And it all stems from the universal need to be needed.

PEOPLE NEED TO KNOW THEY NEED PEOPLE.

"It marks a big step in your development when you come to realize that other people can help you do a better job than you could do alone," said steel magnate and philanthropist Andrew Carnegie. Sadly, many people never achieve that level of maturity or insight. Some people still want to believe that they can achieve greatness alone.

Every individual's fate is tied to that of many others. We cannot be like the shipwrecked man who sits at one end of a lifeboat doing nothing while everyone at the other end bails furiously, and says, "Thank God that hole isn't in *my* end of the boat!" We all need people, and if we don't know it, we're in trouble.

PEOPLE NEED TO KNOW THEY ARE NEEDED.

Cartoonist Charles Schulz often captured the longings of the human heart in his comic strip *Peanuts*. He really understood the needs of people. In one of his creations, Lucy asks Charlie Brown to help with her homework. "I'll be eternally grateful," she promises.

"Fair enough. I've never had anyone be eternally grateful before," replies Charlie. "Just subtract 4 from 10 to get how many apples the farmer had left."

Lucy says, "That's it? That's it? I have to be eternally grateful for that? I was robbed! I can't be eternally grateful for this—it was too easy!"

With a blank look of discouragement, Charlie replies, "Well, whatever you think is fair."

"How about if I just say 'thanks, bro'?" replies Lucy.

As Charlie leaves to go outside, he meets Linus, who asks, "Where've you been, Charlie Brown?"

"Helping Lucy with her homework."

"Did she appreciate it?" Linus asks.

Charlie responds, "At greatly reduced prices."

Ever felt like Charlie Brown? You're not alone. Every

human being longs for a life of significance. We all need to know we are needed and that what we offer to others is of value.

PEOPLE NEED TO KNOW THAT THEY HELPED.

Whenever someone tells me how valuable the people on my team are to them, I encourage him to tell the individuals who were so helpful. Why? Because people need to know that they helped someone. "Good leaders make people feel that they're at the very heart of things, not at the periphery," says author and leadership expert Warren Bennis. "Everyone feels that he or she makes a difference to the success of the organization. When that happens people feel centered and that gives their work meaning."

> "Good leaders make people feel that they're at the very heart of things, not at the periphery."
> —WARREN BENNIS

Walter Shipley of Citibank says, "We have 68,000 employees. With a company this size, I'm not 'running the business' . . . My job is to create the environment that enables people to leverage each other beyond their own individual capabilities . . . I get credit for providing the leadership that got us there. But our people did it." Shipley understands what successful leaders know: people need to know that they made an important contribution to reaching the goal.

It's not a sign of weakness to let others know you value them. It's a sign of security and strength. When you're honest about your need for help, specific with others about the value they add, and inclusive of others as you build a team to do something bigger than you are, everybody wins.

LES ... ON BRINGING IT HOME

Research proved long ago that when people feel needed, they are far more likely to be productive and creative. In fact, studies of twins with similar IQ scores show that each performs quite differently when they are in differing environments, one supportive (where they know they are needed and appreciated) and the other not. The person who feels needed consistently performs better.[1]

To apply John's teaching to your own life . . .

Forget about:
A prideful attitude that causes you to prove how capable you are without the help of others.

Ask:
Who specifically can help me do a better job than I can do alone? Who is just waiting to be asked to join in what I am doing?

Do it:
Sincerely ask others for input or help and attend carefully to what they have to say.

Remember:
Individuals who win with people make others feel that they are at the very heart of things, not at the periphery.

4

CREATE A MEMORY AND
VISIT IT OFTEN

Memory is the treasury and guardian of all things.
—CICERO

∽

LES ... ON SEEING THE PRACTICE IN ACTION

People who spend quality time with John know that they are
going to walk away with a memory. It's inevitable. John just
has a knack for making memories; it's one of the things that
makes him a winner with people.

John also enjoys it when others create a memory for
him. One day when we were talking about creating memories, told me this story: he was scheduled to speak to three
thousand young leaders in Phoenix at an event, but as he
stepped onto the platform that day, he realized his host had
something different in mind. "He didn't want me to speak at
all," John explained. The group that was gathered had been

reading his books and listening to his tapes through the years and had planned a surprise. Instead of having John speak to them, they wanted to speak to John, so they had him sit on the platform and simply listen as they honored him. One after another, twelve preselected leaders from the audience came up to the podium to tell the group about how John's teaching had made an impact on his or her life.

"It was completely unexpected," John said. "And not only did they shower me with kind words, but each speaker presented me with a memento—a tangible remembrance of something they said they had learned from me. I was completely overwhelmed by the experience."

One person gave John a beautiful painting with two images: one of a child reading one of John's books and another of the child as a grown man coaching others.

"Les," John said, tears in his eyes and his voice cracking, "I don't know how many times I've reminisced about that day. I keep the mementos around my office to relive it. That experience meant so much to me. And it renewed my desire to create memories for others."

JOHN . . . WITH A MAXWELL MENTORING MOMENT

Few things bond people together like a shared memory. Soldiers who battle together, teammates who win a championship, and work teams that hit their goals share a connection that never goes away. Married couples who experience rough times can often look back on their earlier experiences together to keep them going. Families bond when they rough it on camping trips or share adventures on vacation and then love recounting their experience years later.

Some memories come as the result of circumstance, but many can be proactively created. Author Lewis Carroll wrote, "It's a poor sort of memory that only works backward." What does that mean to you and me? The richest memories are often those we plan and intentionally create. Here are some hints for creating memories that will help you win with people:

INITIATIVE—MAKE SOMETHING HAPPEN

Memories don't find us—we find them. Even better, if we are intentional, we can *make* memories. If you mention the word *chariot* to friends Dan and Patti Reiland or Tim and Pam Elmore, I can tell you exactly what will come to mind—a crisp autumn day in New York City when we did something that still makes us laugh. After lunch at Tavern on the Green, I hired three "bicycle chariots" with peddling drivers to take each couple on a race through Manhattan to Macy's. It was up to each couple to motivate their driver to win (using whatever financial incentives they wanted). The race was neck-and-neck the entire way, and we laughed the whole time.

We still laugh when we think about it or look at the photos we took that day. But it never would have happened if we hadn't initiated it.

TIME—SET ASIDE TIME TO MAKE SOMETHING HAPPEN

For years parents have debated the issue of quality time versus quantity of time. As a father and grandfather, I have discovered that it takes quantity time to find quality time. If you don't carve out the time, you can't create the memory.

Haven't you found that most memories you have are with the people you spend the most time with? I know that's true for me. If you want to make memories with your family, spend more time with them. If you want to create memories with your employees, you won't do it behind the door of your office. You simply can't make memories with people if you don't take time to be with them.

PLANNING—PLAN FOR SOMETHING TO HAPPEN

Most people don't lead their lives—they accept their lives. They wait for memorable experiences to happen, never giving a thought to planning an experience that will make a memory. One of the most extravagant memories I ever planned was with Margaret, my wife, for our twenty-fifth wedding anniversary. We decided to share it with thirty of our closest friends. We chartered a yacht and picked everyone up in San Diego Bay. Once on board, we had a delectable meal and then surprised the group by having Frankie Valens entertain us with some of his trademark songs like "Sixteen Candles." Our friends loved it. But the most memorable highlight of the evening was created when Margaret and I said a few words about each person and why that person held such a special place in our hearts. That night is not only a great memory for Margaret and me, but it is a great memory for the people who attended, too.

> Most people don't lead their lives—they accept their lives.

28

CREATIVITY—FIND A WAY TO MAKE SOMETHING HAPPEN

What do you do when you find yourself at an event where you expect to share a memory but nothing seems to happen? You get creative. I've been asked over and over to tell the story of the Holiday Bowl I attended in San Diego with friends about fifteen years ago. The game was so dull that I ended up buying newspapers for everyone in my section so that we would have something to do. Another guy nearby, not to be outdone, bought one hundred bags of peanuts and distributed them to everybody in the section. The two of us got a standing ovation, and soon the news crews were more focused on us than the game. I don't remember the score or much about the game, but it's a night I'll never forget. Neither will the buddies who went with me.

SHARED EXPERIENCES—MAKE SOMETHING HAPPEN TOGETHER

Memories compound when they are experienced with someone you love. Years ago our family went to Jasper Park in Canada for a vacation. While we were there, I took my children, Elizabeth and Joel Porter, fishing. On our way back to our cabin, we called Margaret to let her know we were coming home, and she asked the kids how they did.

"We caught eight trout," Joel said. He was acting low-key about it, but I could tell he was proud. As we drove back, we talked about how great it was going to be to have a dinner of trout we had just pulled from a cold mountain stream. When we arrived, we carried the trout into the kitchen, and there on the counter we saw four steaks ready to be cooked.

"What gives?" Joel asked his mother. "We caught eight trout! And we're looking forward to a trout dinner."

Margaret started to laugh. "I thought you said *a* trout, so I went out and bought steaks." Then I started laughing, and Elizabeth did too. Finally, with a gleam in his eye, Joel said, "Mom's not too good with numbers, is she?"

That happened with our kids when they were eleven and thirteen years old. Every time we've had a cookout since then, the kids have told the trout story. Even now that both of them are married and have kids of their own, they still love to say, "Mom's not too good with numbers," and make us laugh.

MEMENTOS—SHOW THAT SOMETHING HAPPENED

"Almost anything you do today will be forgotten in just a few weeks," says author and research scientist John McCrone. "The ability to retrieve a memory decreases exponentially unless boosted by artificial aids such as diaries and photographs."

Don't you find that to be true? Do you keep pictures or souvenirs on your desk where you can see them? Do you carry photos of people you love in your wallet? Do you have a trophy, plaque, game ball, or other award on a shelf where you and others can see it? We all have things we love—not because they have any material value but because they remind us of places we've been or things we've done. When you help someone else create a memory, give that person something to remember it by.

RELIVE THE MEMORY—TALK ABOUT WHAT HAPPENED

The most important part of creating a memory is reliving it. It's the payoff! Many times when I travel with others, at the end of our trip I ask them to share a favorite memory. It often leads to rich conversations. Or I write a note to someone soon afterward to share my own favorite memory. It creates a connection that bonds us together and makes both of us feel great.

LES ... ON BRINGING IT HOME

There isn't a person in the world who doesn't understand the value of positive memories. They can sustain people during the worst of times and inspire them during the best of times. And best of all, anyone can create a memory and visit it often!

To apply John's teaching to your own life . . .

Forget about:

Trying to have quality time to make a memory if you aren't willing to invest the quantity of time it requires.

Ask:

What memories have I already created with people in my life that we need to relive together?

Do it:

Plan an experience that will commemorate an achievement or milestone that people will talk about years from now. And don't forget to create a memento of it.

Remember:

We shouldn't wait for memories to happen to us. We need to make memories happen.

5

COMPLIMENT PEOPLE IN FRONT OF OTHER PEOPLE

Admonish thy friends in secret, praise them openly.
—PUBLILIUS SYRUS

LES ... ON SEEING THE PRACTICE IN ACTION

Complimenting people in front of other people is a John Maxwell trademark. He's known for doing this far and wide. So when I asked a few people around his company to tell me how John does this, I didn't have to look far for stories. Instead, I had to decide which of numerous ones to choose. Many of these stories contained sentiments similar to the ones I heard from Charlie Wetzel, who has worked with John on his books for more than a decade:

For almost twenty years, John has written and recorded leadership lessons, which he used to mentor tens of thousands of people every month, first for the Injoy Life Club and now for Maximum Impact. In 1995, he did a lesson that was designed to teach leaders how to find people with great potential and how to create an environment for them to flourish and emerge as full-fledged leaders. He called it "Searching for Eagles."

John now often records such lessons on-site at corporations and other organizations around the country. But at that time he delivered the teaching to his own church staff and a few people from Injoy, the leadership development company he founded. It was his way of continually developing his people so that they would grow and learn. I sat in the audience that day and took notes as I learned the ten marks of an eagle:

1. Eagles make things happen.
2. Eagles see and seize opportunities.
3. Eagles influence the opinions and actions of others.
4. Eagles add value to you.
5. Eagles draw winners to them.
6. Eagles equip other eagles to lead.
7. Eagles provide ideas that help the organization.
8. Eagles possess an uncommonly great attitude.
9. Eagles live up to their commitments and responsibilities.
10. Eagles show fierce loyalty to the organization and the leader.

It was an inspiring and instructive message. As John wrapped up the lesson, he named some of the eagles that had come into his life through the years. And then John said, "But I want to finish this lesson by telling you about another eagle who has come on board recently. His name is Charlie Wetzel. He's only been working with us a short time, but he makes things happen."

John went on to tell how a connection I made on my own initiative with the editor of a national publication led to the acceptance of a Maxwell article that would be read by over three million subscribers. John then said so many kind and complimentary things about me that it brought tears to my eyes.

John had always said positive things about me in front of my wife and my visiting parents, but this time he was speaking to the entire staff of my church and the president of his company—not to mention the thousands of people who would be listening to the message on tape. It was overwhelming. Before that moment, I'd never thought of myself as an "eagle." Even to this day, it touches my heart when I think about it.

It's been a decade since John paid Charlie that compliment, yet its impact hasn't lessened. That's the power of complimenting people in front of other people.

JOHN ... WITH A MAXWELL MENTORING MOMENT

The most fundamental and straightforward way of winning with people is to give them a compliment—a sincere and meaningful word of affirmation. If you want to make others feel like a million bucks, you've got to master this elementary skill. And it's essential that you learn to give your compliments in front of others as well as one-on-one. Why? Because that private compliment turned public, instantly and dramatically increases in value. Here are reasons why that's so important:

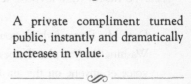

A private compliment turned public, instantly and dramatically increases in value.

People Want to Feel Worthwhile in Life

"Everyone has an invisible sign hanging from his neck," says Mary Kay Ash. "It says, 'Make Me Feel Important!'" Mary Kay drilled this principle into her sales team. She told them again and again, "Never forget this message when working with people." She knew compliments and affirmation were critical to enjoying success with others.

And by the way, it's one of the reasons she was so successful. With her life savings of $5,000 and the help of her then twenty-year-old son, she launched Mary Kay Cosmetics in 1963. The company now has more than 500,000 independent beauty consultants in twenty-nine markets worldwide, and Mary Kay Inc., is ranked as one of the 100 best companies to work for in America.

Mary Kay, like every other person who wins with people, knew that people want to feel worthwhile. When you continually keep this in mind, you can't help but give compliments freely.

COMPLIMENTS INCREASE IN VALUE WHEN WE VALUE THE PERSON WHO GIVES THEM

Willard Scott, the former longtime weatherman on NBC's *Today Show*, remembers his radio days when he received his all-time favorite letter from a fan:

> Dear Mr. Scott, I think you're the best disc jockey in Washington. You play the best music and have the nicest voice of anyone on the air. Please excuse the crayon— they won't let us have anything sharp in here.

Not all compliments are created equal. Who gives the compliment has a lot to do with how much we prize it. A nice remark from someone who's not allowed to have sharp objects doesn't carry the same weight as a compliment given by your boss in front of people you respect.

COMPLIMENTS AFFIRM PEOPLE AND MAKE THEM STRONG

To affirm is to make firm. An affirmation is a statement of truth you make firm in a person's heart when you utter it. As a result, it cultivates conviction. For example, when you compliment a person's attitude, you reinforce it and make it more consistent. Because you notice it in a positive way, he will be more likely to demonstrate that same attitude again.

Likewise, when you affirm people's dreams, you help their dreams become more real than their doubts. Like the repetition of a weight-lifting regimen, routine compliments build up people's qualities and strengthen their personalities.

"There are high spots in all of our lives," wrote author George Matthew Adams, "and most of them have come about through encouragement from someone else. I don't care how great, how famous or successful a man or woman may be, each hungers for applause. Encouragement is oxygen to the soul. Good work can never be expected from a worker without encouragement. No one can ever have lived without it."

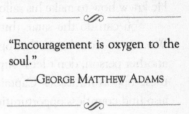

"Encouragement is oxygen to the soul."
—GEORGE MATTHEW ADAMS

COMPLIMENTS IN FRONT OF OTHERS ARE THE MOST EFFECTIVE ONES YOU CAN GIVE

As commander of a $1 billion warship and a crew of 310, Mike Abrashoff used grassroots leadership to increase retention rates from 28 percent to 100 percent, reduce operating expenditures, and improve readiness. How did he do it? Among other things, he placed supreme importance on public compliments.

"The commanding officer of a ship is authorized to hand out 15 medals a year," he wrote. "I wanted to err on the side of excess, so I passed out 115." Nearly every time a sailor left his ship for another assignment, Captain Abrashoff gave him or her a medal. "Even if they hadn't been star players, they got medals in a public ceremony as long as they had done their best every day. I delivered a short speech describing how much we cherished the recipient's friendship, camaraderie, and hard work." Sometimes the departing sailor's shipmates told funny stories, recalling his or her foibles, trials, and triumphs. But the bottom line was that Abrashoff wanted to make them feel good by complimenting them in front of others.

"There is absolutely no downside to this symbolic gesture," said Abrashoff, "provided it is done sincerely without hype." He knew how to make his sailors feel like a million bucks.

You can do the same thing for the people around you. Whenever you have the opportunity to publicly praise another person, don't let it slip by. Of course, you can create these opportunities, as Captain Abrashoff did, but you can also find countless opportunities if you just look for them.

LES . . . ON BRINGING IT HOME

Think about the last time you received a compliment in the presence of people who mattered to you. How did it make you feel? Few things can lift a person up the way a sincere compliment does.

To apply John's teaching to your own life . . .

Forget about:
Giving compliments only in private. Instead, give public praise whenever you can.

Ask:
Who can I spotlight in front of others?

Do it:
Compliment someone around you in front of other people today.

Remember:
When you give someone a public compliment, you give him or her wings like an eagle.

6

GIVE OTHERS A REPUTATION TO UPHOLD

*Treat a man as he appears to be and you make him worse.
But treat a man as if he already were what he potentially
could be, and you make him what he should be.*
—GOETHE

LES...ON SEEING THE PRACTICE IN ACTION

A few years ago, John and Margaret went to London with friends Dan and Patti Reiland, Tim and Pam Elmore, and Andy Stimer. While there, each person had his own must-see destination. For Tim, it was the bunker and war room that Winston Churchill and his advisors used during World War II.

John told me about his experience there. It was not an impressive place: it was basically a basement about twelve feet beneath a building containing a big map room with a large table, a communication room, and some smaller rooms where people could rest. But what had occurred there during the war was impressive. It was from there that Churchill had strategized and rallied the British people.

As we talked, I could tell that John loves history. He talked about Churchill—one of his leadership heroes—and how the prime minister helped to uplift millions of his countrymen in the wake of Britain's June 1940 defeat at the battle of Dunkirk. John quoted part of the speech Churchill used to address the House of Commons upon that occasion:

> We shall not flag or fail . . . We shall fight in France, we shall fight in the seas and oceans, we shall fight with growing confidence and growing strength in the air, we shall defend our island, whatever the cost may be, we shall fight on the beaches, we shall fight on the landing grounds, we shall fight in the fields and in the streets, we shall fight in the hills; we shall never surrender . . .[1]

John explained, "Churchill did a lot of remarkable things during the war, but one of the greatest was his continual ability to give the English people a reputation to uphold. He inspired them; he motivated them; he challenged them. And in response they rose to the occasion. They loved him for it."

John has tried to embody this quality. He says that as he interacts with others, he constantly asks himself, *What is special, unique, and wonderful about this individual?* Then he shares it with others. I've seen John do this time after time. About Linda Eggers, his assistant, he says, "She always represents me well." He calls John Hull, the president of EQUIP,

"Mr. Relationship." He tells everyone that Kirk Nowery, the president of ISS, is "the pastor's best friend." And he points out how Doug Carter, the vice president of EQUIP, "never misses an opportunity to tell the EQUIP story." John thinks the best of people and speaks about the fine qualities he sees in them.

JOHN . . . WITH A MAXWELL MENTORING MOMENT

One of the best ways to inspire others and make them feel good about themselves is to show them who they could be. Years ago, a manager for the New York Yankees wanted rookie players to know what a privilege it was to play for the team. He used to tell them, "Boys, it's an honor just to put on the New York pinstripes. So when you put them on, play like world champions. Play like Yankees. Play proud."

When you give someone a reputation to uphold, you give him something good to shoot for. It's putting something that was beyond his reach within his grasp. By speaking to their potential, you help the people around you to "play proud," as the Yankees do. Why is that important? Because people will go farther than they thought they could when someone they respect tells them they can.

If you desire to give others a reputation to uphold, here are suggestions on how to get started:

HAVE A HIGH OPINION OF PEOPLE

The opinions you have of people in your life affect them profoundly. Dr. J. Sterling Livingston, formerly of the

Harvard Business School and founder of the Sterling Institute management consulting firm, observed, "People perform consistently as they perceive you expect them to perform."

A reputation is something that many people spend their entire lives trying to live down or live up to. So why not help others up instead of pushing them down? All people possess both value and potential. You can find those things if you try.

BACK UP YOUR HIGH OPINION OF OTHERS WITH ACTION

When you back up your belief in people with action, their self-doubt begins to evaporate. It's one thing to tell your teenager that you believe he's a good driver; it's another to let him have the keys to your car for the evening. Likewise, if you want a new manager to rise to the high opinion you've expressed about her, then give her significant responsibility. Nothing gives people confidence like seeing someone they respect put his money where his mouth is. Not only does it empower them emotionally, but it also resources their drive toward success.

LOOK PAST THEIR PASTS AND GIVE THEM REPUTATIONS FOR THEIR FUTURES

Old negative names, labels, or nicknames can block a person's growth and progress. Perhaps that's why the rites of passage in many cultures include giving a new title or name to the person being honored. A new name gives someone a hope for a new future.

A fun example of this can be found in the movie and play *The Man of La Mancha*, based on Cervantes's classic work *Don Quixote*. The protagonist, Don Alonzo, pursues a life of chivalry and seeks to become a knight-errant long after that age of history has passed. He sees giants where others see windmills and quests where others see rabbit trails. Comically, he "rescues" a common prostitute named Aldonza, whom he sees as a beautiful lady. He calls her Dulcinea and makes her the object of his knightly exploits.

At first she resents him. She thinks he is mocking her, because she hates herself and her life. But with time, his vision of her replaces her own and gives her hope. And as the old man lies on his deathbed, she thanks him for seeing in her what she could not see in herself.

Of course, the most dramatic examples of someone overlooking the pasts of others and giving them reputations for the future can be found in the Bible. The book of Genesis recounts how God changed the life of Abram, an old man with no offspring. God renamed him Abraham,[2] which means "father of many," and made it possible for Abraham to become a father in his old age. And God took Jacob, a trickster who cheated his brother, lied to his father, and constantly schemed to get ahead; and renamed him Israel—his future becoming the inception of the nation of Israel.[3]

GIVE PEOPLE A NEW NAME OR NICKNAME THAT SPEAKS TO THEIR POTENTIAL

Harry Hopman, one of the finest tennis captains and coaches in Australia's history and a member of the International Tennis Hall of Fame, at one time built the Australian team to the point that it dominated the tennis world. How did he do it? By emphasizing what he called "coaching by affirmation." For example, he had a slow player whom he nicknamed "Rocket." Another player, who was not known for his strength or constitution, he called "Muscles." And it certainly gave them a boost. "Rocket" Rod Laver and Ken "Muscles" Rosewall became champions in the tennis world.

I love giving people nicknames that speak to their potential and their greatest strengths. In fact, it's something I'm known for in my family. My own children, Elizabeth and Joel Porter, I call "Apple of My Eye" and "Number One Son." I call my nieces Rachael and Jennifer "Angel" and "Sweet Pea." Grandchildren Madeline, Hannah, John Porter, and Ella are "Sunshine," "Hannah Banana," "JP," and "Peanut."

Each time a child is born in our extended family, the kids want to know what I'm going to call the newest member. It's a tradition we all love. Why? Because everyone enjoys the encouragement that comes from someone seeing—and speaking to—their potential.

LES . . . ON BRINGING IT HOME

I sometimes encounter leaders who believe you shouldn't stroke people's egos by giving them reputations they haven't quite earned. And I always point these folks to the "ten-year rule." It's derived from research showing that elite performers, those whose reputations precede them, usually needed at least ten years of dedicated and consistent practice before they obtained any *recognizable* level of excellence. The research also shows that the process can be cut dramatically when individuals see signs that they are already beginning to achieve a recognizable reputation.[4]

To apply John's teaching to your own life . . .

Forget about:

A person's failures in the past and focus on his or her potential in the future.

Ask:

What is special, unique, and wonderful about this person? How can I show it to others?

Do it:

Back up your high opinion of a person with action that reinforces that opinion.

Remember:

Many people go farther than they thought they could go because someone else believed they could and told them so.

7

SAY THE RIGHT WORDS AT THE RIGHT TIME

No man has a prosperity so high or firm, but that two or three words can dishearten it; and there is no calamity which right words will not begin to redress.
—RALPH WALDO EMERSON

LES . . . ON SEEING THE PRACTICE IN ACTION

Ask nearly anyone who knows John well, and he will tell you a story of a specific time when John said the right words to him at the right time. One of the most touching I heard while working on this book came from Dan Reiland, John's close friend and former right-hand man. "John has done this so often in my life," explained Dan. "But the time that stands out above all the others is when my mother died."

Her death was sudden and unexpected. Dan promptly got word to John, who was out of town at the time. John and

Margaret quickly changed their plans and flew back home to San Diego. Dan recalled, "John and Margaret came in the door of our house in Rancho San Diego, walked right up to me, gave me a big hug, and said, 'I love you.' That was it. There's nothing anyone could have done that would have been better." Dan told me that John also said many wise things to his brother, Lan, and greatly encouraged his sister, Jean. I could tell that Dan was still touched by it even though it had occurred nearly a decade ago.

"And John gave a beautiful memorial service," remembered Dan. "He gave me his notes afterward, which I cherish. I value everything John did during that time, but nothing quite holds the power of those three words at that very moment when he walked through that door."

People who have not been around John "up close and personal" are sometimes surprised to find out how good he is at saying the right words at the right time. They're used to his public persona as a speaker, where he also excels at communication and timing. But what they may not realize is that John is a genuine encourager who loves to help people and who really understands them, both on- and offstage.

I remember hearing John speak to an audience of managers about the value of what we say and when we say it. He said . . .

- ◆ The *wrong words* said at the *wrong time* discourage me.
- ◆ The *wrong words* said at the *right time* frustrate me.
- ◆ The *right words* said at the *wrong time* confuse me.
- ◆ The *right words* said at the *right time* encourage me.

I've certainly found that to be true in my own life. Haven't you? The right words at the right time are like a soothing breeze of encouragement.

JOHN . . . WITH A MAXWELL MENTORING MOMENT

Most people recognize that words have incredible power. Editor and theologian Tyron Edwards observed, "Words are both better and worse than thoughts; they express them, and add to them; they give them power for good or evil; they start them on an endless flight, for instruction and comfort and blessing, or for injury, sorrow and ruin." But saying the right words is not enough. Timing is crucial.

Sometimes, the best thing we can do for someone else is to hold our tongue. When tempted to give advice that's not wanted, to show off, to say "I told you so," or to point out another's error, the best policy is to say nothing. As nineteenth-century British journalist George Sala advised, we should strive "not only to say the right thing in the right place, but far more difficult, to leave unsaid the wrong thing at the tempting moment."

When it is time to speak up, how can you best encourage others using the right words at the right time? Keep these thoughts in mind:

BE SENSITIVE TO TIME AND PLACE

It's said that during one of the last major offensives of World War II, General Dwight Eisenhower was walking near the Rhine and came upon a GI who seemed depressed.

"How are you feeling, son?" he asked.

"General," the young man replied, "I'm awful nervous."

"Well," Eisenhower said, "you and I are a good pair then, because I'm nervous too. Maybe if we just walk along together, we'll be good for each other."

The first key to saying the right thing at the right time is paying attention to the context. That is one of the secrets of successful communication to a large audience, and it is just as important when talking with someone one-on-one. King Solomon of ancient Israel was speaking to this truth when he wrote, "Like apples of gold in settings of silver is a word spoken in right circumstances."[1] If you can learn to be sensitive to your setting, you've won half the battle in saying the right words at the right time.

> "Like apples of gold in settings of silver is a word spoken in right circumstances."
>
> —KING SOLOMON OF ISRAEL

SAY IT FROM THE HEART

It's not just what you say and when you say it: it's also *how* you say it. A *Peanuts* comic strip shows Lucy saying to pianist Schroeder, "Do you think I'm the most beautiful girl in the world?" Naturally, she has to ask several times in different ways, until Schroeder, to be finally rid of her, says, "Yes."

Lucy mopes disconsolately and comments, "Even when he says it, he doesn't say it."

People can tell the difference between hollow words and something that is said from the heart. Idaho businessman Don

Bennett was the first amputee to climb to the summit of Mount Rainier. That's 14,410 feet, on one leg and two crutches! During an especially difficult portion of the climb, Bennett and his team had to cross an ice field. To get across the ice, the climbers had to put crampons on their boots, which would give them traction. Unfortunately, one boot didn't help Bennett much. The only way he could get across the ice field was to fall face forward onto the ice, pull himself as far forward as he could, stand up, and then fall forward again.

Bennett's teenage daughter, Kathy, was with him on the climb. She stayed by his side through the entire four-hour struggle. She kept cheering him on, saying, "You can do it, Dad. You're the best dad in the world. You can do it!"[2] His daughter's words, spoken from the heart, helped him to keep going.

RECOGNIZE THE POWER OF THE RIGHT WORDS AT THE RIGHT TIME

Saying the right words at the right time can do more than just make a person feel good in the moment. It can have an impact that is positive and lasting.

Painter Benjamin West said that he loved to paint as a youngster. When his mother left the house, he would get out the oils and try to paint. One day when he pulled out paints, brushes, paper, and various other implements, he made quite a mess. When he realized his mother would be home soon, he tried desperately to get everything cleaned up, but he didn't make it. When she walked into the room, he expected the worst.

West said that what she did next completely surprised him. She picked up his painting, looked at it, and said, "My, what a beautiful painting of your sister." She gave him a kiss on the cheek and walked away. With that kiss, West said, he became a painter.

I don't know what kind of experience you had growing up. Perhaps, like me, you had parents who understood the power of encouragement. If not, what would you have given to have someone speak into your life at the right time—a parent, teacher, coach, or pastor? Whether or not you received it then, you can give it now. Look for opportunities to uplift others with your words. It just might change their lives.

LES . . . ON BRINGING IT HOME

Numerous studies back up that when you say the right words at the right time, there are a number of positive outcomes. One of the most important outcomes is trust. When you can offer something to a person at the point of his or her need—even when that person is a stranger—you are very likely to become trusted and seen as honorable. You will be seen as someone who is dependable and considerate.[3] Isn't that encouraging?

To apply John's teaching in your own life . . .

Forget about:
What you want to say and focus on what the other person needs to hear.

Ask:
What would I want to hear if I was in this person's shoes?

Do it:

Change someone's day—or maybe even his entire life—by saying the right words at the right time, from the heart.

Remember:

"Like apples of gold in settings of silver is a word spoken in the right circumstances."

8

ENCOURAGE THE DREAMS OF OTHERS

Keep away from people who try to belittle your ambitions. Small people always do that, but the really great make you feel that you, too, can become great.

—MARK TWAIN

LES... ON SEEING THE PRACTICE IN ACTION

When I began talking to John's office staff, one of the things I found out is that he receives dozens of letters every week thanking him for the positive changes that have come as a result of his books, seminars, and lessons on CD. I asked Sue Caldwell if I could see some of the letters, and she handed me a thick folder that contained some that she had shared with the staff. As I flipped through the pages, I noticed how many times people had written about hopes and dreams being rekindled in them.

Two letters jumped out at me because they referred to

things that occurred at a conference for young Christian leaders at which John had spoken. The first, from Kevin, said:

> Thank you! Without being overly dramatic, I cannot begin to tell you how much value you have added to my life over the past six years. I was one of the 5,500 emerging leaders who attended "Catalyst" this past week . . . I feel like God answered my prayer as you poured out your heart to us during your session . . . You said, "I wish you believed in yourself as much as I believe in you." That is the first time I have heard that from anyone in your generation. It was tremendously empowering to hear.

The second one, written by Matt, said:

> Over the past few months, I had become very discouraged and resigned myself to the fact that the dream [I had previously pursued] was dying. Then I came to Catalyst '03. Totally unexpectedly to me, God moved in my heart and reassured me His plan was still alive. When you prayed over us during the session, I could not stop weeping. Your words were directly from God's heart to mine. I will never forget that moment . . . Thanks for impacting my life.

Matt went on to say that he had rededicated himself to his dream and would persevere during this preparation period of his life.

As I talked to John's employees and associates, I discovered that he had repeatedly encouraged their dreams, even when that meant he might lose someone he valued. Often when Tim Elmore—a pastor on John's staff in San Diego for more than ten years—was recruited by another organization, he would go to John and ask him to "take off his employer hat and put on his mentor hat" so that he could ask John's advice. Tim says that John could be remarkably objective, and several times he actually encouraged Tim to pursue it, saying, "This just might be a good fit for you. I don't want you to have regrets if you don't go and see about it. I think you should go."

One of those trips eventually took Tim away when he accepted a position as a vice president of a parachurch organization in Colorado. And John was nothing but encouraging. He truly wanted Tim to realize his dreams and fulfill his potential.

JOHN ... WITH A MAXWELL MENTORING MOMENT

I consider it a great privilege when people share their dreams with me. It shows a great deal of courage and trust. And at that moment, I'm conscious that I have great power in their lives. That's no small matter. A wrong word can crush a person's dream; the right word can inspire him or her to pursue it.

If someone thinks enough of you to tell you about his or her dreams, take care. And keep these things in mind as you work to encourage that person:

UNDERSTAND THAT DREAMS ARE FRAGILE

Actress Candice Bergen commented, "Dreams are, by definition, cursed with short life spans." I suspect she said that because there are people who don't like to see others pursuing their dreams. It reminds them of how far they are from living their own dreams. As a result, they try to knock down anyone who is shooting for the stars. By talking others out of their dreams, critical people excuse themselves for staying in their comfort zones.

> "Dreams are, by definition, cursed with short life spans."
> —CANDICE BERGEN

Never allow yourself to become a dream killer. Instead, become a dream releaser. Even if you think another person's dream is far-fetched, that's no excuse for criticizing them.

To Lose a Dream Is a Great Loss

Have you given up on one of your dreams? Have you buried a hope that once looked bright and gave you energy? If so, what did it do to you? Norman Cousins, former editor of the *Saturday Review* and adjunct professor of psychiatry at UCLA, believed, "Death is not the greatest loss in life. The greatest loss is what dies inside of us while we live."

> "Death is not the greatest loss in life. The greatest loss is what dies inside of us while we live."
> —NORMAN COUSINS

Our dreams keep us alive. Benjamin Franklin observed, "Most men die from the neck up at age twenty-five because they stop dreaming." That's why it's so important that you help keep others' dreams alive. By doing so, you can literally help them live. Encouraging another person's dream can nurture her soul.

ENCOURAGING OTHERS IN THEIR PURSUIT OF A DREAM IS TO
GIVE THEM A WONDERFUL GIFT

Because dreams are at the center of our souls, we must do
everything in our power to help turn dreams into reality.
That is one of the greatest gifts we can ever give. How can
you do it? Follow these six steps:

1. *Ask them to share their dream with you.* Everyone has a
   dream, but few people are asked about it.

2. *Affirm the person as well as the dream.* Let the person
   know that you not only value his or her dream but
   that you also recognize traits in that individual that
   can help him or her achieve it.

3. *Ask about the challenges they must overcome to reach their
   dream.* Few people ask others about their dreams; even
   fewer try to find out what kinds of hurdles the person
   is up against to pursue them.

4. *Offer your assistance.* No one achieves a worthwhile
   dream alone. You'll be amazed by how people light up
   when you offer to help them achieve their dream.

5. *Revisit their dream with them on a consistent basis.* If you
   really want to help others with their dreams, don't
   make it a one-time activity you mark off your list.
   Check in with them to see how they're doing and to
   lend assistance.

6. *Determine daily to be a dream booster, not a dream buster.*
   Everyone has a dream, and everyone needs encouragement. Set your mental radar to pick up on others'
   dreams and help them along.

PEOPLE WILL LIVE UP TO THEIR DREAMS WHEN THEY HAVE A CHANCE TO FULFILL THEM

Scott Adams, creator of the popular *Dilbert* cartoon, tells this story about his beginnings as a cartoonist:

> You don't have to be a "person of influence" to be influential. In fact, the most influential people in my life probably are not even aware of the things they've taught me. When I was trying to become a syndicated cartoonist, I sent my portfolio to one cartoon editor after another—and received one rejection after another. One editor even called and suggested that I take art classes. Then Sarah Gillespie, an editor at United Media and one of the real experts in the field, called to offer me a contract. At first, I didn't believe her. I asked if I'd have to change my style, get a partner—or learn how to draw. But she believed I was already good enough to be a nationally syndicated cartoonist. Her confidence in me completely changed my frame of reference and altered how I thought about my own abilities. This may sound bizarre, but from the minute I got off the phone with her, I could draw better.

Editor Sarah Gillespie gave Adams a chance to live out his dream, but because so many people had tried to discourage him, he was almost afraid to say yes. But because of her encouragement—and the opportunity she gave him—*Dilbert* has become one of the most popular cartoons in the nation.

There is no telling what might happen if you were to begin encouraging the dreams of the people around you. When you come to the end of your life, wouldn't you love to be the person about whom others say, "I succeeded because this person believed in me when nobody else did"? Start encouraging others. The more you do, the more they will share their dreams with you. And the greater the chance you will get to watch them bloom.

LES ... ON BRINGING IT HOME

In case you fear that encouraging people's dreams will simply cause them to keep their heads in the clouds, research reveals that this practice does more than cause individuals to seek something positive in the future. It actually causes them to be more engaged in their present activities. Technically speaking, it's called the "resonance performance model," but whatever you call it, you can't go wrong by encouraging the dreams of others.

To apply John's teaching to your own life . . .

Forget about:
Critiquing another person's dream. Instead, affirm his lofty vision and his pursuit to realize it.

Ask:
Who can I encourage today in reaching their dreams?

Do it:
Offer specific help in bringing another person closer to making his or her dream a reality.

Remember:
When a person shares his or her dream with you, it is the center of that person's soul.

9

PASS THE CREDIT
ON TO OTHERS

If each of us were to confess his most secret desire,
the one that inspires all his plans, all his actions,
he would say: "I want to be praised."
—E. M. CIORAN

LES . . . ON SEEING THE PRACTICE IN ACTION

One of my favorite topics of conversation with John is publishing. We've talked about it for nearly two decades now. Whether book ideas, titles, marketing campaigns, publishers, bookstore shelf space, or agents, we have bandied about nearly every conceivable aspect of the industry. And since John has been one of the most successful authors in the area of leadership and sold more than nine million books, I'm always intrigued to learn about the ins and outs of his publishing experiences.

Some time ago John and I were both speaking at a conference in Virginia, and between sessions I asked him to pinpoint a publishing highlight in his career.

"That's a tough one, Les," he told me. "I've been blessed in ways I could have never anticipated."

"Surely something stands out," I gently pressed.

"Well, when *The 21 Laws of Leadership* sold one million copies, Thomas Nelson, the publishing house, hosted a celebration banquet for about 120 people from their company and Injoy to mark the occasion. They gave me some beautiful gifts that night, including these." John pulled up the sleeve of his jacket and pointed to the gold cuff links he was wearing, each bearing the number "21." "What an honor that evening was."

Sometime later, I spoke to a few of the people who attended that banquet, including John's wife, Margaret. She said that when John got up to address everyone, he expressed his gratitude and quickly started crediting the people who had helped make it happen. He told how Victor Oliver had come up with the original concept for the book and had provided the title. He credited a group of key leaders at Injoy who had helped him hone the laws. He thanked Charlie Wetzel, his writer, for being the book's wordsmith. He thanked Ron Land of Thomas Nelson and Kevin Small and the Injoy team for putting together the book tour that helped put *The 21 Laws* on the *New York Times*'s best-seller list. He thanked publisher Mike Hyatt, the Nelson sales and marketing staff, the booksellers, and many other individuals, including his parents. Margaret said that by the time John finished, there wasn't a dry eye in the room.

Making a book successful and getting it into the hands of

people it can help is always a team effort, though not all authors see it that way. Everybody involved in the process has a part to play, and John did his best to pass along the credit by recognizing each person's contribution.

JOHN ... WITH A MAXWELL MENTORING MOMENT

I'll never forget that night in Orlando. When I wrote my first book in 1979, I never dreamed that anything I wrote would sell a million copies. As Margaret and I went back to our hotel room, she asked me what I considered to be the highlight of the banquet. Without hesitation I replied that it was passing on the credit to the people who helped me so much. Rarely do we get an opportunity to say thank you enough to the people who help us, especially in such a public setting. I really wanted to make the most of it. Not only does it make me feel good to share any success I might have, but it uplifts others—and it makes them feel like a million bucks.

Passing the credit on to others is one of the easiest ways to win with people. If you'd like to practice it, here are a few suggestions to get you started:

CHECK YOUR EGO AT THE DOOR

The number one reason people don't pass along credit to others is that they think it will somehow hurt them or lessen their value. Many people are so insecure that they constantly feed their egos to compensate for it. But you simply cannot practice this method of winning with people if you can't set your ego aside.

Have you ever heard the saying "An egotist is not a person who thinks too much of himself; it's someone who thinks too little of other people"? If you want to give others credit, put your focus on others. What do they need? How will giving them credit make them feel? How will it enhance

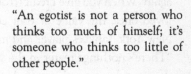

"An egotist is not a person who thinks too much of himself; it's someone who thinks too little of other people."

their performance? How will it motivate them to reach their potential? If you highlight their contributions, it makes them *and* you look good.

DON'T WAIT—PASS THE CREDIT ASAP

I love what H. Ross Perot once said about passing on credit: "Reward employees while the sweat's still on their brow." Isn't it true that one of the very best times to give credit to others is when the amount of work and sacrifice something took is still fresh in their minds? Why wait? You may have heard management expert Ken Blanchard's teaching that you should catch people while they're doing something good. What a great idea! The sooner you give credit to someone else, the bigger the payoff.

In 2003, when I interviewed UCLA basketball coach John Wooden, he told me how he would often teach his players who scored to give a smile, wink, or nod to the player who gave them a good pass. "What if he's not looking?" asked a team member. Wooden replied, "I guarantee he'll look." Everyone enjoys having his contribution acknowledged.

SAY IT IN FRONT OF OTHERS

You've already read the chapter that encourages you to compliment people in front of other people, but it bears saying again. When you give credit to others in front of their peers and loved ones, the value of your compliment multiplies. Former New York Yankees player and manager Billy Martin observed, "There's nothing greater in the world than when somebody on the team does something good and everybody gathers around to pat him on the back." By giving credit in a crowd, you can help to create the kind of environment Martin described.

PUT IT IN PRINT

When you give people credit verbally, you uplift them for a moment. When you take the time to put it in writing, you have the potential to uplift them for a lifetime. People put plaques on their walls as reminders of their achievements. They save and cherish letters containing recognition and praise for things they've done. Deep down, everyone wants to make a difference, and some days, everyone is in need of some encouragement.

I have a file in my office with letters and notes that have special significance for me. Every now and then, I'll pull out the file and read some of the things people I respect have told me. It allows me to relive that moment of encouragement. It's said that even President Abraham Lincoln used to carry in his pocket a newspaper clipping extolling his accomplishments as president. He was one of the finest leaders in our nation's history, yet he desired something to keep his spirits up.

Please don't underestimate the impact that an article, a public notice, or a personal note can make. What takes you only a few minutes to write may be something that inspires another person for decades.

ONLY SAY IT IF YOU MEAN IT

I love this old joke: As an old man lay dying, his wife of many years sat close by his bed. He opened his eyes and saw her. "There you are, Agnes," he said, "at my side again."

"Yes, dear," she replied.

"Looking back," the old man said, "I remember all the times you were by my side. You were there when I got my draft notice and had to go off to fight in the war. You were with me when our first house burned to the ground. When I had the accident that destroyed our car, you were there. And you were at my side when my business went bankrupt and we lost every cent we had."

"Yes, dear," his wife said.

The old man sighed.

"I tell you, Agnes," he said, "you've been a real jinx."

It may seem obvious, but I want to go ahead and say it anyway so that I'm not misunderstood. You should never say something you don't believe just to uplift someone. If you're not sincere, you don't make people feel good; you make them feel they're being schmoozed. When you pass credit on to others, you need to do it from the heart.

LES . . . ON BRINGING IT HOME

Passing credit along to coworkers or colleagues is more than mere niceness. According to research, when you pass credit along to others, you actually change their biochemistry and create an "emotional stamp" that forever associates you in their minds with their success.

To apply John's teaching to your own life . . .

Forget about:

Your ego. Focus on the people around you and the credit they deserve.

Ask:

Who has made me more successful than I would have been on my own?

Do it:

Publicly pass along credit for a successful endeavor to as many people as you can.

Remember:

If each of us were to confess our most secret desire, we would say: "I want to be praised."

10

OFFER YOUR VERY BEST

I do the very best I know how—the very best I can;
and I mean to keep on doing so until the end.
—ABRAHAM LINCOLN

LES . . . ON SEEING THE PRACTICE IN ACTION

For many years now I've received the leadership lessons on tape and CD that John does every month. After listening to one titled "Preparation: The Separation Between Winning and Losing," I had to ask John a question.

"I loved the teaching, and I pulled some nuggets from it that have really helped me," I said, "but I need to ask you a question. Do you really believe preparation is that important in a person's life?"

"Absolutely," John answered. "It really does make the difference between winners and losers. Preparation is more than just a discipline. It's an attitude, a way of life. My father used to quote the Bible verse that says, 'Whatever your hands find to do, do it with all your might.' In other words, in what you do, in what you have, offer your very best. I try to embrace that in everything I do."

I've watched John for years, and I believe that's true. Everything he does, he does with excellence. But it's also more than that. While we were working on this book, we had a meeting in San Diego where John was spending some time while awaiting the birth of his fourth grandchild. When we were done, John took us to dinner at his favorite restaurant in San Diego—Peohe's, which has excellent food and an even better view. It's on Coronado island and is situated on the bay across the water from San Diego's beautiful skyline.

The hostess seated us outside right by the water, and John and Margaret immediately took the two seats facing the restaurant so that everyone else in the party could enjoy the view of the bay. During our meeting earlier in the day in an ocean-view room, John had also sat with his back to the window, allowing others who were visiting from other parts of the country to enjoy the view. And neither time had it been by accident. I know John: he always thinks through what's going to be happening at a meeting and picks his seat carefully. He had taken the worst seat because he wanted to offer all of us the very best.

JOHN ... WITH A MAXWELL MENTORING MOMENT

For years I've been invited to be the keynote speaker for organizations at their special events. It's something I really enjoy. Communicating to an audience energizes me. It would be easy for me to "wing it" or do a canned speech that I have done elsewhere before. But I never do that because I don't believe it would serve them well. Instead, I spend time researching the company. I find out as much as I can about the particular event they've planned and what they desire to accomplish. You may wonder why I would go to such trouble when I don't necessarily need to. I do it because I have a goal every time I speak. After I'm done communicating with the audience, I want the person who invited me to speak at the event to say, "You exceeded our expectations." I want to deliver for them . . . and then some.

Perhaps you are someone who already possesses an offer-your-best mind-set. If so, I commend you, and I want to encourage you to maintain that attitude. If not, I hope the following thoughts will help you develop that mind-set:

ANYONE CAN BE AN IMPORTANT PERSON TO ME

We are most likely to give our best to those we love and respect. I think back to my days in school, and I remember loving some teachers and having others who left me cold. I know that I always did my best for the teachers I liked, and for the others I did only what was needed to get a grade. Later, I realized that my off-and-on efforts frequently hurt my relationships with others as well as my potential for success. But then I discovered the antidote: if I saw *everyone* as important—not just the people I liked the most—I would always offer my very best. That change in attitude prompted a change in my actions.

ANYTHING WE DO CAN BE MADE IMPORTANT

Most moments in life become special only if we treat them that way. The average day is average only because we don't make it something more. The most excellent way to elevate an experience is to give it our best. That makes it special. An average conversation becomes something better when you listen with great interest. A common relationship transforms when you give it uncommon effort. An unremarkable event becomes something special when you spice it up with creativity. You can make anything more important by giving your best to it.

YOU CAN BECOME IMPORTANT TO ANYONE

Who are the most important people in your life? Are they the ones who never give you the time of day, who never seem to be there when you need them? Of course not. Usually the people who are important to you are the ones who treat *you* as important. We naturally value the people who value us. So if you want to be important to others, treat *them* as important. The most effective way to do that is to give them your very best.

MAKE THE MOST OF YOUR GIFTS AND OPPORTUNITIES

More than thirty years ago I memorized a quote that has shaped the way I live: "My potential is God's gift to me. What I do with my potential is my gift to Him." I believe I am accountable to God, others, and myself for every gift, talent, resource, and opportunity I have in life. If I give less than my best, then I am shirking my responsibility. I believe UCLA coach John Wooden was speaking to this idea when he said,

"Make every day your masterpiece." If we give our very best all the time, we can make our lives into something special. And that will overflow into the lives of others.

There's a story I love about President Dwight Eisenhower. He once told the National Press Club that he regretted not having a better political background so that he would be a better orator. He said his lack of skill in that area reminded him of his boyhood days in Kansas when an old farmer had a cow for sale. The buyer asked the farmer about the cow's pedigree, butterfat production, and monthly production of milk. The farmer said, "I don't know what a pedigree is, and I don't have an idea about butterfat production, but she's a good cow, and she'll give you all the milk she has." That's all any of us can do—give all that we have. That's always enough.

> "My potential is God's gift to me. What I do with my potential is my gift to Him."

LES . . . ON BRINGING IT HOME

A tremendous amount of recent psychological research has focused on the value of virtues. And experts are finding that when people strive toward excellence in character traits—for example, when they work to possess a giving spirit—they routinely benefit themselves while in the process of benefiting others. This is known in the field as cultivating "fulfillments."[1] One hardly needs a research study, however, to know that when you give your very best, you are bound to feel fulfilled.

To apply John's teaching to your own life . . .

Forget about:

Doing the minimum required to get by, and focus instead on your maximum effort.

Ask:

What can I do for someone who could never repay me?

Do it:

Voluntarily give beyond what is required.

Remember:

Everybody appreciates a person who gives his very best.

11

SHARE A SECRET
WITH SOMEONE

*Conceal not your secret from your friend,
or you deserve to lose him.*
—PORTUGUESE PROVERB

LES . . . ON SEEING THE PRACTICE IN ACTION

In 1996 John made a major decision concerning his company, and for a time let only a few people in on it. Charlie Wetzel was one of them. Here's what Charlie has to say about what that did for him and his relationship with John:

> One day John asked me to come up to his home office so that we could work on our current book project. We had a very productive work session, and after we were done, John said, "Charlie, before you go, I want to talk to you about something."

When an employee hears those words from his boss, he takes notice. Sometimes the words that follow include the phrases "tough economy," "poor performance," or "you're fired!"

John continued, "In about twelve months, we're going to move the company out of San Diego. We're not going to announce it to all the staff yet, but I'm telling the people on the executive team—my inner circle—about the move so that they can begin processing the information. We're going to be moving to Atlanta."

John went on to explain that flying out of San Diego was taking its toll, not only on him, but also on the consultants who worked for the company. When John had asked his assistant, Linda Eggers, to calculate how many days he spent the previous year just making flight connections from San Diego to Dallas, Chicago, or Atlanta, Linda came back with a mind-boggling figure: thirty days! That's when John knew he had to make a move.

That was a lot of information, so I started processing it. Then John said, "Charlie, I sure hope you'll come with us."

John spoke to me for probably only two minutes, but what he communicated changed my life. At that time I had been working with John for about two years, and we had already written five or six books together. I had worked hard for him, and John had always been lavish with his praise. But I had no idea he valued me as much as he did. Once he shared this secret, my place in his estimation, in my career, and even in my own eyes changed.

John has done a lot of wonderful things for my family and me through the years. He is very generous, and many of those things have cost him a lot of time and money. Sharing the secret of our move cost him nothing, yet it made a huge impact on me. It made me feel like a million bucks.

It's not a secret how powerful sharing with another person can be. It's a surefire way to win with people.

JOHN ... WITH A MAXWELL MENTORING MOMENT

A Sicilian proverb says, "Only the spoon knows what is stirring in the pot." When you allow another person to know what is stirring within you, giving him a "taste" of a plan or idea, you instantly make a meaningful connection with him. Who doesn't want to know what's going on in the mind of someone they care about?

Reading Charlie Wetzel's story might make you think that sharing a secret with someone always has to be a big deal with life-changing ramifications. It doesn't. Of course, when you let people in on something impacting, it makes quite an impression. But you can make sharing a secret part of your everyday life using everyday things. The first time you share something with others, aren't you sharing something that has been secret up to that moment? Why not let the person to whom you're talking know that you're revealing it for the first time? That makes him feel special.

Sharing a secret with someone is really a matter of two things: reading the context of a situation and desiring to build up the other person. If you do those two things, you can learn this skill. As you try it out, keep these three things in mind:

1. SHARING A SECRET MEANS GIVING VALUABLE INFORMATION.

When you share a secret, the information needs to be something that the people you're talking to care about. It plays to their interests or meets a felt need they possess. For example, two experienced deep-sea fishermen decided to go ice fishing. They each chopped holes in the ice, put worms on their hooks, dropped their lines into the water, and waited. After three hours, they had caught nothing.

As they sat, they watched a boy come along and cut a hole in the ice midway between them. He put a worm on his hook, dropped his line into the water, and almost instantly he caught a fish. The boy repeated the process and quickly had a catch of more than a dozen fish. The two other fishermen watched and were flabbergasted.

Finally, one of the men approached the boy and said, "Young man, we've been here for more than three hours and haven't caught a single fish. You've caught at least a dozen in just a few minutes. What's your secret?"

The boy mumbled an answer, but the man didn't catch a word of it. Then he noticed a large bulge in the boy's left cheek. "Please, could you take the bubble gum out of your mouth so I can understand what you're saying?" the man said.

The boy cupped his hands, spat it out, and said, "It's not bubble gum; it's my secret. You've got to keep the worms warm."

2. SHARING A SECRET MAKES PEOPLE FEEL SPECIAL.

Letting people in on something always boosts their egos. Charlie's comment says it all: "I had no idea he valued me as much as he did. My place in his estimation, in my career, and even in my own eyes changed." But as I said, the secret doesn't always have to be dramatic to have a positive effect. For example, when I play golf, I usually carry a laminated card with me that contains tips given to me by golf pro Scott Szymoniak. Occasionally if a friend in the group is not playing well, I'll pull him aside and say, "I want to share a secret with you that has really helped my golf game." Then I'll pull out the card and show him the six basic things a golfer must know and do. And I'll let him know that it's my personal golf plan and that I don't share it with everybody.

How does it make you feel when you know that you're the first person being told something? I know it makes me feel special. That's one of the reasons my wife, Margaret, and I have practiced telling each other first about many of the things that happen to us during the day. To help me do that, I carry a note card or small pad and jot down things I want to tell her. Anything I write down I "save" to tell her first. It leads to special times together every day.

3. SHARING A SECRET INCLUDES OTHERS IN YOUR JOURNEY.

The bottom line on sharing a secret with others is that it is an act of inclusion. It invites others into your life, into your experience. It includes them in your success. When I speak to an audience—whether it's a roundtable of executives or an arena full of people—I intentionally use inclusive language. I let people in on my personal journey. And when I'm revealing something I've not previously

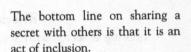

The bottom line on sharing a secret with others is that it is an act of inclusion.

said publicly, I let them know that I'm doing so. It communicates to people that I care about them and want to help them.

LES ... ON BRINGING IT HOME

When people are "in the know," according to research, a slew of positive attributes are correlated with their lives. For example, they are far more likely to feel that their jobs fit their ambitions. They are more likely to be active in public service. They have patterns of rich friendships and happier marriages. Researchers call this an "adaptive mental mechanism."[1]

Whatever terminology you use, it turns out that when you share a secret with others, you are doing far more than imparting mere information. You are increasing the odds of a closer relationship.

To apply John's teaching to your own life ...

Forget about:
Hoarding information for yourself.

Ask:
Whom can I benefit most by letting them in on some otherwise private information?

Do it:
Find someone to let in on a secret today.

Remember:
Sharing a secret with someone is bound to boost their self-esteem.

12

MINE THE
GOLD OF GOOD
INTENTIONS

To err is human; to forgive is not company policy.
—UNKNOWN

LES . . . ON SEEING THE PRACTICE IN ACTION

Do you ever struggle to give people the benefit of the doubt—to mine the "gold" of their good intentions? I know I do. Especially when I think they've dropped the ball or tried to hurt me. But if you're like me, you also know that this tendency can be a costly interpersonal mistake if you want to win with people. So when I confessed this faux pas to John one day, he immediately identified with what I said. But he also told me how he had learned to give people the benefit of the doubt: he watched his mother.

"Mom knew my heart and she always evaluated my behavior in light of it," John explained. "Today when I say to someone, 'I didn't mean to do that,' I often wish that they would 'mine the gold of my good intentions' like my mom did. Her ability and willingness to do this in my life was a tremendous gift—and it's helped me to give the benefit of the doubt to others."

"Are you saying your mom looked past all your mistakes?" I asked.

John laughed. "Definitely not. Like every other kid, I got my fair share of reprimands. And trust me, I deserved them! But Mom never seemed to jump to conclusions with me. She never assumed the worst. Instead, she always assumed the best. And that's key to cultivating this quality.

"You see," John continued, "it did so many things for me." He counted them off: "It allowed me to draw close to her. It made her approachable. It brought out the best in me. And it taught me how to do this for others."

"Okay, John," I asked as I considered his words, "do you think that a person who wasn't raised in a home where this kind of quality was modeled is going to have a tougher time doing this for others?"

"Les, I don't really think so," he said. "Sure, a person whose home life wasn't positive won't have seen it modeled, so that person may not do it *naturally*. But when it comes right down to it, giving others the benefit of the doubt is a choice. And I've seen a lot of people who grew up with few advantages rise above that and become winners in every sense of the word."

That gives everyone hope.

JOHN . . . WITH A MAXWELL
MENTORING MOMENT

Let's start by being honest. Not everyone has pure intentions. If you mine the gold of good intentions, occasionally people will take advantage of you. They have in my life. And they will in the future. But because I assume the best in others, so many people have done so many wonderful things for me I literally cannot count them all.

I've found that when I am suspicious of others, it causes me to display wrong behavior toward them. And it actually makes any interaction with them worse. In general, you get what you expect from others. So I have chosen to take the high road, expect the best, and be blessed most of the time. If you desire to do the same, do the following:

BELIEVE THE BEST ABOUT PEOPLE

The first thing you need to do is check your attitude. How do you see others? Do you believe that, deep down, every person desires to be good, to do his best? That matters, because if you don't believe the best in others, you will never believe that their intentions are good. And if you don't believe in their intentions, I imagine you will not exert the effort to "mine" the gold that is in them.

SEE THINGS FROM THEIR PERSPECTIVE

The issue of perspective really has to do with maturity. Consider the story of two Cub Scouts whose younger brother had fallen into a lake. They rushed home to Mother with tears in their eyes. One of them sobbed, "We tried to give him CPR, but he kept getting up and walking away."

Without maturity, we lack perspective. The less mature one is, the more difficult it is to see things from another's point of view. Think about the biblical story of the woman caught in adultery where Jesus challenged the people without sin to cast the first stone. The *oldest* people in the crowd were the first to drop their stones and walk away. Why? Their maturity gave them better perspective.[1]

"Since we tend to see ourselves primarily in light of our *intentions*, which are invisible to others," said philosopher J. G. Bennett, "while we see others mainly in the light of their *actions*, which are all that's visible to us, we have a situation in which misunderstanding and injustice are the order of the day." And that's precisely why the ability to see things from another's perspective is essential to finding the gold of their good intentions.

GIVE PEOPLE THE BENEFIT OF THE DOUBT

When you were a child, perhaps you were taught the Golden Rule: "Do unto others as you would have them do unto you." I've often found that when my intentions were right but my action turned out wrong, I wanted others to see me in light of the Golden Rule. In other words, I wanted others to give me the benefit of the doubt. Why shouldn't I try to extend the same courtesy to others?

Frank Clark commented, "What great accomplishments we would have in the world if everybody had done what they intended to do." While I'd agree that's true, I'd also add, "What great relationships we would have if everybody was appreciated for what they intended to do—in spite of what they may have done." When you give someone the benefit of the doubt, you are following the most effective interpersonal rule that has ever been written.

"Since nothing we intend is ever faultless, and nothing we achieve without some measure of finitude and fallibility we call humanness, we are saved by forgiveness."

—DAVID AUGSBURGER

REMEMBER THEIR GOOD DAYS, NOT THEIR BAD ONES

We all have good days and bad days. I don't know about you, but I'd like to be remembered for my good ones. And I can only ask to be forgiven for my bad ones. Fuller Theological Seminary Professor David Augsburger observes, "Since nothing we intend is ever faultless, and nothing we achieve without some measure of finitude and fallibility we call humanness, we are saved by forgiveness." If you desire to mine the gold of good intentions in others, then forgiveness is essential. And it's rarely a one-time thing. Civil rights leader Martin Luther King Jr. was right when he said, "Forgiveness is not an occasional act; it is a permanent attitude."

"Forgiveness is not an occasional act, it is a permanent attitude."

—MARTIN LUTHER KING JR.

And remember, it is with the attitude with which you judge others that you will also be judged. If you mine the gold of good intentions in your relationship with others, then people will more likely do the same for you.

LES . . . ON BRINGING IT HOME

If you grew up in an environment where the worst was assumed about you instead of the best, take heart. A research study that followed children for thirty years found that exceptional and caring adults often emerged from difficult childhoods. What made the difference? Two qualities stood out: (1) they found a nurturing relationship somewhere along the line—whether it was a mentor or other kind of role model, and (2) they had a desire to help other people.[2]

To apply John's teaching to your own life . . .

Forget about:

Justice; instead, focus on grace and forgiveness.

Ask:

How would I feel and what would I do if I were in this person's shoes?

Do it:

Practice the Golden Rule by appreciating what others intend, not only what they do—just as you would like for them to do with you.

Remember:

If I fail to believe the best in others, I will not give the effort to "mine" the gold contained in them.

13

KEEP YOUR EYES OFF THE MIRROR

*I don't know what your destiny will be,
but one thing I know: the only ones among you who
will be really happy are those who have sought and
found how to serve.*

—ALBERT SCHWEITZER

LES ... ON SEEING THE PRACTICE IN ACTION

Soon after John relocated his companies from San Diego, California, to Atlanta, Georgia, in 1997, he hired researcher George Barna to fly to Atlanta and do some strategic planning with the executive team. Barna is the leading director of the Barna Group, a full-service marketing research company located in Ventura, California. Their expertise is in tracking cultural trends and collecting information on the Christian church.

The leaders and top thinkers from John's companies gathered together in the conference room for an all-day session where they could ask Barna anything they wanted to help them plan business and marketing strategies for the next several years. It took everyone no time at all to dive in and begin picking Barna's brain. He answered question after question. They brainstormed concepts and strategies. And they bounced ideas off of Barna to see if he thought they would fly.

Linda Eggers, John's longtime assistant, noticed that during the long sessions, John listened attentively but rarely chimed in. He seemed content to just listen. At the end of the day, when she and John sat down to attend to calendar items, correspondence, travel arrangements, and the like, Linda noticed that John had an entire legal pad of questions for George Barna that he had never asked.

Linda was surprised—especially since she had booked Barna and she knew exactly how much John had paid for the consultation.

"John, you just let everyone else talk today," she remarked. "Why didn't you ask him any of *your* questions?"

"You know what, Linda?" John said. "Everybody was obviously very excited about meeting with George, and it was so energizing to them, I didn't want to do anything to ruin the momentum. It doesn't matter that I didn't get my questions answered. Some other time."

Linda says that is one of the reasons she loves working for John. "I know that because he seems larger than life and has such charisma in front of an audience," Linda said, "there are people out there who think he has a big ego. They have no idea how much he thinks about others and puts them first."

If you focus on others, continually working to give them what they need, then you are able to keep your eyes off the mirror. And that's a wonderful way to win with people.

JOHN ... WITH A MAXWELL MENTORING MOMENT

One of the key questions I ask in my book *Winning with People* is the Connection Question: Are we willing to focus on others? The foundational concept for that question is the Big Picture Principle, which states: "The entire population of the world—with one minor exception—is composed of other people." If you've never thought of life in those terms, then it's time to give it a try. If individuals think they are the center of the universe, not only are they in for a big disappointment when they discover it's not true, but they'll also alienate themselves from everyone around them. I've never met a person that truly wins with other people who has not mastered the ability to keep his eyes off the mirror and serve others with dignity.

Most people would readily admit that unselfishness is a positive quality, and even the most egocentric individual possesses the desire, deep down, to help others. The problem, sometimes, is changing our behavior so that we get in the habit of focusing on others instead of on ourselves. Here are a few thoughts to help you remember to keep your eyes off the mirror:

FOCUSING ON OTHERS CAN GIVE YOU A SENSE OF PURPOSE

If you grew up in the 1950s and '60s, you may remember Danny Thomas, the entertainer who starred in the TV show *Make Room for Daddy*. Thomas observed, "All of us are born for a reason, but all of us don't discover why. Success in life has nothing to do with what you gain in life or accomplish for yourself. It's what you do for others."

Not only did Thomas believe that, but he also lived it. As a successful entertainer and television star, he could have done nothing but enjoy the benefits of his achievement. But he desired something more. He founded St. Jude's Hospital, a research facility that focuses on treating children who suffer from catastrophic diseases. And Thomas dedicated much of his life to supporting it. It helped him enjoy a greater purpose.

FOCUSING ON OTHERS CAN GIVE YOU ENERGY

Continual focus on yourself can actually drain you of energy, while focusing on others can have the opposite effect. My friend Bill McCartney knew this back when he was head football coach for the University of Colorado Buffaloes. Coach Mac had heard that most people spend 86 percent of their time thinking about themselves, but only 14 percent of their time thinking about others. Yet he knew instinctively that if his players focused their attention on someone they cared about instead of just on themselves, a whole new source of energy would be available to them.

In 1991 Coach Mac decided to use this information when he was facing a great challenge. Colorado was scheduled to play its archrival, the Nebraska Cornhuskers, on Nebraska's home turf. The problem was that Colorado had not won a game there in twenty-three years. But Coach McCartney believed in his team and looked for a way to inspire them to achieve. In the end, he decided to appeal to their love of others.

He did it by challenging each player to call an individual he loved and tell that person he was dedicating the game to him or her. Coach Mac also encouraged the players to ask that person to watch every play, knowing that every hit, every tackle, every block, and every score was being dedicated to him or her.

Coach Mac also took one more step. He arranged to distribute sixty footballs with the game's final score written on them, so that each player could send a ball to the individual he had chosen.

The Colorado Buffaloes won the game. The final score written on the footballs was "27 to 12."

Focusing on Others Can Give You a Sense of Contentment

I'm told that psychological research shows that people are better adjusted and more likely to feel content if they serve others. Serving others actually cultivates health and brings about happiness. People have instinctively known that for centuries—even before the science of psychology was formally developed. For example, look at the wisdom (and humor) found in this Chinese proverb:

If you want happiness for an hour—take a nap.
If you want happiness for a day—go fishing.
If you want happiness for a month—get married.
If you want happiness for a year—inherit a fortune.
If you want happiness for a lifetime—help others.

You can actually *help yourself* by helping others.

Remember that, and it will help you to take—and keep—your eyes off the mirror.

LES . . . ON BRINGING IT HOME

Some researchers call it the "ultraself" and consider it the hallmark of wisdom. It refers to a sense of serenity that allows one to focus on others from an emotionally secure place. It is free from petty jealousy and competitiveness. It takes genuine joy in another's success. And study after study shows it to be one of the most important ways to make meaningful connections with others.[1]

To apply John's teaching to your own life . . .

Forget about:
Trying to find happiness by tending to your own needs first.

Ask:
What can I do to forget myself and focus on others?

Do it:
Set your needs aside and do something specific, today, that will help you keep your eyes off the mirror.

Remember:
Success in life has everything to do with what you do for others.

14

DO FOR OTHERS WHAT THEY CAN'T DO FOR THEMSELVES

You have not lived today until you have done something for someone who can never repay you.

—JOHN BUNYAN

LES . . . ON SEEING THE PRACTICE IN ACTION

Early on, John gave a boost to my speaking career when he opened doors I could have never opened myself. On his recommendation, I was standing on speaking platforms around the country, addressing audiences of several thousand at a time. The people who booked the events didn't know me; they knew John and trusted his endorsement of a young speaker who was just getting started.

That was fifteen years ago, and I'm just as grateful now for what John did for me in those early days as I was when it first happened. John gave me something that I could have never gotten without him—a launch to my professional speaking career.

Countless people could tell stories of how John extended himself in some way to help them along personally or professionally. When I talked to Tim Elmore, a longtime friend and employee who is now a vice president of EQUIP, he said, "It's hard for me to narrow it down. John has done so many things for me, and I owe him so much."

He thought for a moment and then told me this:

Maybe something more personal will really show you John's heart. John and I were in Bangalore, India, to teach leadership—a trip, I might add, that I would not have gotten to take if John hadn't hired me at EQUIP. Before we left the country, my wife, Pam, asked John to keep an eye on me because I'm diabetic. If my blood sugar level drops suddenly, I get disoriented, I have no clue that I'm getting into trouble physically, and I usually need to go to a hospital for help. It can be scary—especially when you're overseas.

When we got to India, John was received like a rock star! You wouldn't believe the way people treated him. Overseas, people wait in lines literally for hours to meet him and have him sign his books. Anyway, John taught a session in Bangalore, and the crowd was going nuts, and the people were all crowding around him, and what does he do? He pushes his way through the crowd, grabs the kit with my diabetic supplies, and checks up on me to make sure I'm not in trouble.

That probably sounds like a small thing but it's hard to

believe that anybody would not get caught up in that kind of moment and would instead focus on somebody else's needs. It really reveals John's heart and desire to do for others.

Tim got choked up as he told me the last part. I was touched by his story. But there's something that made an even greater impression on me. All the people I talked to about this quality in John said that they desired to do for others what John did for them. Because they have been helped to do things they otherwise couldn't do on their own, they're inspired to give others a boost.

JOHN ... WITH A MAXWELL MENTORING MOMENT

Ambassador and poet Henry Van Dyke observed, "There is a loftier ambition than merely to stand high in the world. It is to stoop down and lift mankind a little higher." What a great perspective! Doing for others what they can't do for themselves is really a matter of attitude. I believe that whatever I've been given is to be shared with others. And because I have an abundance mind-set, I never worry about running out myself. The more I give away, the more I seem to get to give away.

No matter how much or how little you think you have, you have the ability to do for others what they cannot do for themselves. Exactly how you do that will depend on your

> "There is a loftier ambition than merely to stand high in the world. It is to stoop down and lift mankind a little higher."
>
> —HENRY VAN DYKE

unique gifts, resources, and history. However, you can approach the task by thinking in terms of four areas:

1. INTRODUCE OTHERS TO PEOPLE THEY CAN'T KNOW ON THEIR OWN.

My dad, Melvin Maxwell, has done many incredible things for me during the course of my life. One of the things that impacted me most was his introducing me to great men. As a teenager, I met Norman Vincent Peale, E. Stanley Jones, and other exceptional men of the faith. And because I had declared my intention to go into the ministry, my father asked these preachers to pray for me. I can't express in words what that did for me.

Today, I am often in a position to do for others what my father did for me. I love introducing young people to my heroes. I love helping people make business contacts. There are often times when I meet someone, and as we talk, it just hits me: I need to introduce this person to so-and-so. That can mean walking somebody across the room, making a phone call on his or her behalf, or arranging a meeting. Several years ago, I was talking to Anne Beiler, the founder of Auntie Anne's, the pretzel company, and she mentioned in passing that Chick-fil-A's founder, Truett Cathy, was one of her heroes. Since I knew Truett, I offered to introduce them to each other. I hosted a dinner party for them at my house, and it was a great night.

Please don't get the impression that you have to know someone famous to help others in this area. Sometimes it's as simple as introducing one friend to another or one business associate to another. Just make connections. Be the bridge in people's relationships with others.

2. TAKE OTHERS TO PLACES WHERE THEY CAN'T GO ON THEIR OWN.

Early in our marriage, Margaret and I were dirt poor. Right out of college, I put in long hours for my career, and Margaret worked three jobs for us to make ends meet. And we did manage to get by, but there was no money left over for luxuries, such as vacations. Fortunately, I had an older brother who loved us and took care of us. The first five or six years of my professional life, any vacation we took was at the invitation of Larry and his wife, Anita. A wonderful trip to Acapulco, Mexico, especially stands out in my mind.

It seems that during the first half of my career, if I got to go anywhere of value to me, it was because someone invited me. Dozens of times I've had experiences that I could not have gained access to on my own: I've gone to ball games, played golf courses, seen churches, attended conferences, and visited countries that appeared to be beyond my reach.

You may have the power to give someone an experience that seems inaccessible to them. If you can't help a friend or colleague, then start with your family. Take your children places they could not go on their own. There's no telling what kind of positive impact it will make.

3. OFFER OTHERS OPPORTUNITIES THEY CAN'T REACH ON THEIR OWN.

Les mentioned that I helped him to reach larger audiences early in his speaking career. The same thing was done for me. Nearly twenty-five years ago, Professor C. Peter Wagner of Fuller Seminary invited me to speak to audiences of pastors around the country about leadership. He put me on a national stage for the first time and gave me credibility that I didn't possess on my own.

Few things are of greater value to a prepared person than an opportunity. Why? Because opportunities increase our potential. Demosthenes, the great orator of ancient Greece, said, "Small opportunities are often the beginning of great enterprises." An opportunity seized is often a source of success. Help people win by giving them opportunities, and you will win with them.

> "Small opportunities are often the beginning of great enterprises."
> —DEMOSTHENES

4. SHARE IDEAS WITH OTHERS THAT THEY DON'T POSSESS ON THEIR OWN.

What is an idea worth? Every product begins with an idea. Every service begins with an idea. Every business, every book, every new invention begins with an idea. Ideas are what make the world move forward. So when you give people an idea, you give them a great gift.

One of the things I love about writing books is the process that it takes me through. It usually starts with a concept that I'm anxious to teach. I get a few ideas down on paper, and then I call together a group of good creative thinkers to help me test the concept, brainstorm ideas, and flesh out the outline. Every time we've done this, people have given me great ideas that I never would have come up with on my own. I have to say I'm very grateful.

One of the things I enjoy most about creative people is that they love ideas, and they always seem to have more coming.

The more they give away, the more new ideas they seem to have. Creativity and generosity feed each other. That's one of the reasons I'm never reluctant to share ideas with others. I'm convinced that I will run out of time long before I run out of ideas. It's better to give some away and contribute to another person's success than to have them lying dormant in me.

LES . . . ON BRINGING IT HOME

When you do something for others that they can't do for themselves, you are fostering relationships with those individuals that are sure to be meaningful. Studies on what researchers call the "self-determination theory" have shown that supporting other people's goals cements the relationship, since you are ultimately helping them to align their goals with themselves.[1]

To apply John's teaching to your own life . . .

Forget about:

Focusing on what you can get from others and focus instead on what you can do for others.

Ask:

What opportunity, idea, or experience could I provide that someone might never be able to have without my help?

Do it:

Consider specific things you might be able to do for others by making a list of your unique skills, resources, and connections.

Remember:
We all need others to do for us what we cannot do for ourselves.

15

LISTEN WITH
YOUR HEART

*The most important thing in communication is
to hear what isn't being said.*
—PETER DRUCKER

LES . . . ON SEEING THE PRACTICE IN ACTION

As a psychologist, I've been trained to listen for people's feelings, not just their ideas. And I've observed that many leaders—especially strong ones with type-A personalities—are not particularly good at listening. When they do listen, their attitude is usually, *Never mind the delivery story, just show me the baby*.

I would consider John to be a pretty strong person. He can be a take-charge, take-no-prisoners kind of leader. But he is also an effective listener. And he's particularly adept at sensing how people feel. Since that characteristic is unusual for most people like him, I asked him how he came to be such a good listener.

"Failure," was his answer. "Repeated failure. I started out as a terrible listener. Early in my career, I thought I knew it all. The only reason I let people talk was that I knew my turn to talk was coming.

"In my marriage, I was a *little* bit better," John continued. "I very much *wanted* to listen to Margaret because of my love for her. However, that didn't stop me from being Mr. Answer Man. In *Winning with People*, I tell about how I used to win arguments but run over her emotionally. Finally, understanding how I was hurting her feelings caused me to stop what I was doing and learn how to listen—not just to the words, but to the feelings behind her words. I learned to listen with my heart."

"So how did you make the transfer from home to your career?" I asked.

"I saw the value in it from the way Margaret's and my relationship changed. But I also came to realize that it was good leadership too. President Woodrow Wilson said, 'The ear of the leader must ring with the voices of the people.' For a couple of years, whenever I was in a meeting, I wrote a large 'L' at the top of my legal pad to remind myself to listen. In time, it became a skill I mastered."

If you are already a good listener, you are ahead of the game. All you have to do is listen "between the lines" for cues that will tell you how others feel. If you're more like John, it may take you some time to learn the skill of listening with your heart. But anyone can do it—you don't need to be a trained psychologist!

JOHN ... WITH A MAXWELL
MENTORING MOMENT

If you are a poor listener, as I was, then do the following to transform yourself into someone who listens with the heart:

FOCUS ON THE PERSON

Herb Cohen, often called the world's best negotiator, says, "Effective listening requires more than hearing the words transmitted. It demands that you find meaning and understanding in what is being said. After all, meanings are not in words, but in people." Many people put their focus on the ideas being communicated, and they almost seem to forget about the person. You can't do that and listen with the heart.

I am naturally very impatient, so I continually have to fight against the tendency to put my agenda first. I think that is often the case with poor listeners. If that is true for you, slow down and put the person first. Focus on the individual, not just the ideas being expressed.

UNCLOG YOUR EARS

Even after you have begun to focus on the person with whom you are conversing, you may still experience many potential barriers to effective listening. Here are a few of them:

Distractions—Phone calls, TV, pagers, and things of that sort can make good listening nearly impossible.

Defensiveness—If you view complaints or criticism as a personal attack, you can become defensive. Once you begin to protect yourself, you will care little about what others think or how they feel.

Closed-mindedness—When you think you have all the answers, you close your mind. And when you close your mind, you close your ears.

Projection—Automatically attributing your own thoughts and feelings to others prevents you from perceiving how they feel.

Assumptions—When you jump to conclusions, you take away your own incentive to listen.

Pride—Thinking we have little to learn from others is, perhaps, the most deadly of distractions to listening. Being full of yourself leaves little room for input from others.

Obviously, your goal is to remove these barriers to good communication. Whenever possible, put yourself in a good physical environment for listening—away from noise and distractions. And also put yourself in a good mental environment for listening—set aside your defenses and preconceived notions so that you are *open* to communication.

LISTEN AGGRESSIVELY

There's a difference between listening passively and listening aggressively. To listen with your heart, your listening has to be active. In his book *It's Your Ship* (Warner, 2002), Captain Michael Abrashoff explains that people are more likely to speak aggressively than to listen aggressively. When he decided to become an intentional listener, it made a huge difference in him and his crew. He wrote:

> It didn't take me long to realize that my young crew was smart, talented, and full of good ideas that frequently came to nothing because no one in charge had ever listened to them. Like most organizations, the Navy seemed to put managers in a transmitting mode, which minimized their receptivity. They were conditioned to promulgate orders from above, not to welcome suggestions from below.
>
> I decided that my job was to listen aggressively and to pick up every good idea the crew had for improving the ship's operation. Some traditionalists might consider this heresy, but it's actually just common sense. After all, the people who do the nuts-and-bolts work on a ship constantly see things that officers don't. It seemed to me only prudent for the captain to work hard at seeing the ship through the crew's eyes. Something happened in me as a result of those interviews. I came to respect my crew enormously. No longer were they nameless bodies at which I barked orders. I realized that they . . . had hopes, dreams, loved ones, and they wanted to believe that what they were doing was important. And they wanted to be treated with respect.

There's a difference between listening passively and listening aggressively. To listen with your heart, your listening has to be active.

As Abrashoff's attitude changed, his crew

transformed, his ship turned around, and the results were astounding.

LISTEN TO UNDERSTAND

The fundamental cause of nearly all communication problems is that people don't listen to understand; they listen to reply. David Burns, a medical doctor and professor of psychiatry at the University of Pennsylvania, says: "The biggest mistake you can make in trying to talk convincingly is to put your highest priority on expressing your ideas and feelings. What most people really want is to be listened to, respected, and understood." If you want to meet others' needs and make them feel like a million bucks, then you need to listen.

One of the ironies of becoming a good listener is that listening to others and making them feel understood also has a side benefit. According to Burns, "The moment people see that they are being understood, they become more motivated to understand your point of view." Listening with the heart produces a win-win situation in relationships.

LES . . . ON BRINGING IT HOME

Few relational topics have had more empirical support than the importance of active listening. Psychologists sometimes call it "listening with the third ear." And the bottom line of most studies shows exactly what John is teaching. When we listen for genuine understanding, we are no longer "playing the role" of listening, but we are fully in the moment, and the person knows it.[1]

To apply John's teaching to your own life . . .

Forget about:

Trying to get your own point across and put your energy into understanding the other person's point.

Ask:

How can I better understand what this person is feeling and thinking?

Do it:

Listen aggressively by eliminating distractions and focusing on the other person's point of view.

Remember:

The best way to persuade is with your ears.

16

FIND THE KEYS TO THEIR HEARTS

*Coaches who can outline plays on a blackboard are a
dime a dozen. The ones who succeed are those who
get inside their players and motivate them.*
—VINCE LOMBARDI

LES . . . ON SEEING THE PRACTICE IN ACTION

When communicators speak to audiences, a funny thing
often occurs. You have a clear purpose in mind, prepare your
message carefully, and deliver it. But when people come up to
you to talk about what you said—each person seems to have
heard a different message. It never fails.

I asked John if he had experienced the same phenome-
non. "Absolutely," he answered. "When I first started preach-
ing, I was surprised. I used to wonder if everybody had heard
the same sermon. In a way, they hadn't. The words I say may

be the same for everyone, but the members of the audience listen differently because they all have different keys to their hearts. That's not only a great lesson for a speaker, but it's also important to remember anytime you work with people."

Whenever I spend time with John, I see him connect with people at the heart level immediately. For example, the other day while I was with him, John met with Kirk Nowery, the president of one of John's companies, ISS. Many times when a leader meets with someone who works for him, he or she immediately gets down to business. But the first thing John did was talk to Kirk about his family. He wanted to know how his wife was doing. He asked about their grown children. John seemed to know all about Kirk's family. And once they had caught up, then they talked business.

John does this intuitively with everyone he knows. He asks about many people's spouses and children by name. He inquires about what's happening at a person's church or business. And he seems to remember the details. Why? Because he makes it his goal to know what's important to the people who are important to him. And by the way, he is able to know these things because he listens with his heart, as we explained in the previous chapter.

JOHN . . . WITH A MAXWELL
MENTORING MOMENT

In the 1980s, I had the privilege, along with about thirty other leaders, to spend two days with the father of modern management, Peter Drucker. One of the things he said was,

"Leading people is like conducting an orchestra. There are many different players and instruments that the conductor must know thoroughly." Drucker challenged us to *really* know the key players on our team.

For the last twenty years, I have purposefully tried to discover the keys to the hearts of the people in my life, starting with the people in my family and my inner circle. Here's what I've learned along the way:

ACCEPT THE FACT THAT PEOPLE ARE DIFFERENT

I've written in previous books about how, when I was young, I used to believe that everyone ought to be like me in order to be successful. I've matured quite a bit since then. Some of my growth has come as a result of traveling and meeting many kinds of people. Books such as Florence Littauer's *Personality Plus* (Revel, 1992) have also helped me. I've come to realize with time that I've got major gaps in my skills and abilities, as everyone does, and if people with different talents and temperaments work together, we all win and get a lot more done. We also enjoy the journey of life much more.

If you have a healthy self-image, you may fall into the same trap I did. However, you cannot win with people if you secretly harbor the belief that everyone ought to be more like you. Accept that people are different, and celebrate that God made us that way.

FIND THE KEYS TO THEIR HEARTS BY ASKING QUESTIONS

It may seem fundamental, but asking a good question is essential to discovering the keys to a person's heart. Through the years, I have developed a list of questions that have helped me in this endeavor time and time again. You may want to use them too:

"What do you dream about?" You can learn about people's minds by looking at what they have already achieved, but to understand their hearts, look at what they dream of becoming.

"What do you cry about?" When you understand people's pain, you can't help but understand their hearts.

"What do you sing about?" What brings people joy is often a source of their strength.

"What are your values?" When people give you access to their values, know that you have entered the most sacred chambers of their hearts.

"What are your strengths?" Whatever people perceive as their strengths makes their hearts proud.

"What is your temperament?" Learn that, and you often discover the way to their hearts.

Obviously, you don't want your questions to feel like an interview, and you don't need to find out all of the answers in one sitting. The process can be natural while being intentional.

ESTABLISH COMMON GROUND

Our English word *communication* comes from the Latin word *communis*, which means "common." Effective leaders, communicators, and people persons always find something they have in common with the people they are speaking to. It is on common ground that they connect with others. If you've asked questions and listened, then you will have discovered common ground.

Sometimes in meetings, hidden agendas can make communication ineffective because they make it difficult for people to meet on common ground. When that happens, try suggesting that all parties agree to a simple little ground rule. When one person disagrees with another, before he's allowed to make his own point, he has to understand and be able to articulate his opponent's point. You would be amazed at how quickly this practice puts people on common ground.

REALIZE THAT WITH TIME, PEOPLE CHANGE

It is a major leap for some people to tune into others' dreams and desires and to discover the keys to their hearts. But it's not enough to do that once with a person and then think you've "got it" forever. Time changes all things, including the human heart.

Fred Bucy, former president of Texas Instruments, observed, "It is much easier to assume that what worked yesterday will work today, and this is simply not true." What's effective in motivating people at one point in their careers will not necessarily be effective in motivating them later. What touches their hearts at one stage of life may not be the same as they grow older. Successes and failures, tragedies and triumphs, goals achieved and dreams laid to rest all make an impact on a person's values and desires.

So what does that mean to someone who wants to win with others by finding the keys to their hearts? It means you should . . .

↪ STAY IN CONTINUAL CONVERSATION WITH OTHERS. Keep connecting on the heart level. Ask about what has touched their hearts up to now; if their responses are different, then you know they are changing, and you have a new opportunity to learn about what matters to them now.

↪ LOOK FOR THE "CHANGE INDICATORS" OF A PERSON'S LIFE. There are certain times in people's lives when they are most likely to change: (1) when they *hurt* enough that they *have to*, (2) when they *learn* enough that they *want to*, and (3) when they *receive* enough that they are *able to*.

If you practice these two disciplines, especially with your family and the key players in your organization, you'll be able to stay connected with them.

I need to tell you one more thing about finding the keys to people's hearts, and this is the most important point: Once you have found a key to a person's heart, you must act with integrity, because you have been entrusted with something of great value. Never use it to manipulate someone. "Turn" the key only when you can add value to that person.

LES . . . ON BRINGING IT HOME

Genuine concern for others is a lifestyle more than a technique. Sure, you can practice the tips John suggests and find immediate benefit, but they will never really pay off in your relationships until you practice them consistently. In fact, research shows that

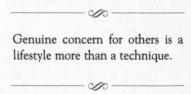

Genuine concern for others is a lifestyle more than a technique.

in learning to develop this quality, you are far more likely to see it become a part of your personality if you work at it on a daily basis, if you make it a reflexive habit with the people around you.[1] In other words, this needs to be something you *are* more than something you *do*.

To apply John's teaching to your own life . . .

Forget about:

Your inclination to believe that everyone is (or should be) just like you.

Ask:

What "change indicators" have I seen in the person whose heart I'd like to understand?

Do it:

Purposefully try to discover the keys to the hearts of your inner circle.

Remember:

Leaders who succeed are those who understand the hearts of their team.

17

BE THE FIRST TO HELP

After the verb "to love," "to help" is the
most beautiful verb in the world.
—BERTH VON SUTTNER

LES ... ON SEEING THE PRACTICE IN ACTION

"Les, where are you?"

"I just passed the Hotel del Coronado, and I'm pulling into the complex," I said.

"What color is your rental car?"

"It's silver," I told John over my cell phone.

"Okay, I can see you coming up right now," John said. "Take an immediate right and you'll see a parking space that is just now opening up."

"Where are you?" I asked.

"Look up." John was standing on a balcony of the high-rise building on Coronado island in San Diego. He had rented a condo, and I had just flown in for a day of meetings with him.

"Oh, there you are!" I started to laugh as I saw him waving at me from the balcony. Only John would think of actually scouting out parking spaces from a bird's-eye view so that he could make it easier for me to find a space.

I've long known that offering help to others is a key to winning with people. It's one of the first lessons you'll pick up in any social psychology class. But John puts a new twist on it. He goes out of his way to be helpful, and when someone's in need, he's often the first on the scene.

"Sometimes it's the little things with John," said employee Ken Coleman. "When I'm traveling with him, I've often seen John help someone struggling to get his or her suitcases into the airplane compartment while most other passengers are oblivious and trying to maneuver around the person. John makes a conscious effort to help in the moment. It seems to be an almost reflexive action with him."

John's twenty-six-year career in ministry probably has made a great impact on him in this area. Good pastors seem able to tune in to people's needs. But you don't have to be a professional shepherd to see people's needs and be the first to help. It's the kind of thing that anyone can do—regardless of age, talent, or socioeconomic status.

JOHN . . . WITH A MAXWELL MENTORING MOMENT

My friend Zig Ziglar said, "You can get everything in life you want if you will just help enough other people get what they want." Zig is certainly living proof of that. He has helped so many people, and he has been a success as a result.

I like helping people. I think it's one of the reasons God put us here on earth. But helping others does more than benefit others. It also helps you win with them. I say that because

> "You can get everything in life you want if you will just help enough other people get what they want."
> —ZIG ZIGLAR

whenever you are quick to help others, it makes a statement. It's like leaving a calling card they will never forget.

So how do you become someone who is the first to help? Follow these guidelines:

MAKE HELPING OTHERS A PRIORITY

We are often so consumed with our own agendas that helping others never becomes important to us. The solution is to make helping others part of your agenda—a top priority. I read recently about something Academy Award–winner Tom Hanks did years ago on the set of *The Green Mile* that shows how helping others is a priority for him. Frank Darabont, director of the film, reflected on Hanks's commitment to helping rising actor Michael Duncan achieve his best, and the impression it had on him. Darabont said:

Fifteen, twenty years from now, what will I remember [about filming *The Green Mile*]? There was one thing—and I'll never forget this: As we're shooting, [the camera] is on Michael Duncan first, and I'm realizing that I'm getting distracted by Hanks. Hanks is delivering an Academy Award–winning performance, off-camera, for Michael Duncan—to give him every possible thing he needs or can use to deliver the best possible performance. He wanted Michael to do so well. He wanted him to look so good. I'll never forget that.[1]

Tom Hanks, like some other Hollywood actors, could have been the first to bail out on Duncan. Instead he was the first to help. It obviously paid off. In 1999, Michael Clarke Duncan was nominated for an Academy Award in the Best Actor in a Supporting Role category. And Duncan's career has since taken off.

MAKE YOURSELF AWARE OF PEOPLE'S NEEDS

This may sound obvious, but you can't meet a need that you don't know exists. Each of us must begin by caring about the people around us and looking for their needs. Sometimes that knowledge can come from listening with your heart. Sometimes it comes from just paying attention to what's going on around you. Other times it comes from mentally putting yourself in another person's place.

There is a Jewish legend that says two brothers once shared a field and a mill, each night dividing the grain they had ground together during the day. One brother lived alone; the other was married with a large family.

One day the single brother thought to himself, *It isn't fair that we divide the grain evenly. I have only myself to care for, but my brother has children to feed.* So each night he secretly took some of his flour to his brother's storehouse.

But the married brother considered his brother's situation, and said to himself, *It isn't right that we divide the grain evenly, because I have children to provide for me in my old age, but my brother has no one. What will he do when he's old?* So every night he secretly took some of his flour and put it in his brother's stores. As a result, both of the brothers found their supply of grain mysteriously replenished each morning.

Then one night they met each other halfway between their two houses. They suddenly realized what the other was doing, and they embraced each other in love. The legend is that God witnessed their meeting and proclaimed, "This is a holy place—a place of love—and here it is that my temple shall be built." The first temple is said to have been constructed on that very site.[2]

BE WILLING TO TAKE A RISK

Sometimes helping another person can be a risky proposition, yet that should not keep us from lending a hand. There's a story Ken Sutterfield tells from the 1936 Olympic Games in Berlin, Germany, that illustrates the impact that can be made by taking such a risk. Coming into the games, American sprinter Jesse Owens had set three world records in one day, including a leap of 26 feet 8 1/4 inches in the running broad jump—a record that would stand for twenty-five years. However, Owens faced great pressure during the games. Hitler and his fellow Nazis wanted to use the competition to establish Aryan superiority, and Owens, a black man, could sense the hostility toward him.

As Owens tried to qualify for the finals during the games, he became rattled as he saw a tall, blue-eyed, blond German taking practice jumps in the 26-foot range. On his first jump, Owens leaped from several inches beyond the takeoff board. Then he fouled on the second attempt. He was allowed only one more attempt. If he missed it, he would be eliminated.

The tall German approached Owens and introduced himself. His name was Luz Long. As the Nazis watched, Long encouraged Owens and offered him some advice: since the qualifying distance was only 23 feet 5 1/2 inches, Long suggested that Owens make a mark several inches before the takeoff board to make sure he didn't foul. Owens qualified on his third jump. In the finals, he set an Olympic record and earned one of his four gold medals. And who was the first person to congratulate Owens? Luz Long!

Owens never forgot the help Long had given him, though he never saw Long again. "You could melt down all the medals and cups I have," Owens wrote, "and they wouldn't be plating on the 24-carat friendship I felt for Luz Long."[3]

Follow Through Once You Begin to Help

Philanthropist Andrew Carnegie was approached by members of the New York Philharmonic Society, one of Carnegie's favorite charities, for financial support. He was about to write a check to wipe out the Society's entire deficit when suddenly he stopped. "Surely there must be other rich, generous music lovers in this town who could help out," he said. "Why don't you raise half this amount, and come back to me for the other half," said the great philanthropist.

The next day, the treasurer came back and told Carnegie that he had raised $30,000 and would like now to get Carnegie's check. The patron of the arts was immensely pleased at this show of enterprise and immediately handed it over. But he was curious. "Who, may I ask, contributed the other half?"

"Mrs. Carnegie," came the reply.

Sometimes when we are the first to offer help, we discover that the person to whom we made the offer isn't in as great a need as we first expected. Follow through anyway. Being the first to help is a great way to win with people. Offering to help and then not following through is a sure way to lose.

LES . . . ON BRINGING IT HOME

Studies on altruism fill volume after volume of academic journals. If there is one thing the professional community of psychologists knows, it's that being helpful is one of the shortest distances between two people—especially when you are the *first* to help. And like John says, helping others speaks volumes about you.[4]

To apply John's teaching to your own life . . .

Forget about:
Thinking only about what's in it for you and think about how you can offer a hand.

Ask:
How can I help you?

Do it:
Be the first to volunteer your services, offer assistance, or lend a hand.

Remember:
If you help enough people get what they want, you'll get what you want too.

18

ADD VALUE TO PEOPLE

*Try not to become a man of success,
but rather try to become a man of value.*
—ALBERT EINSTEIN

LES . . . ON SEEING THE PRACTICE IN ACTION

I've heard John speak to all kinds of audiences all over the globe, and a theme that runs like a ribbon through many of his talks has to do with adding value to people. Whatever the conference or topic, he often weaves the importance of "adding value" into it. I've also been in meetings around a conference table where John focuses on value added—to him from others and by him to others. It's a John Maxwell trademark.

So when I started researching the subject for this book, I went to Dan Reiland, a friend and colleague of John's for more than twenty years.

"John has desired to add value to people for as long as I've known him," said Dan, "but in recent years he has identified that as his primary purpose in life. And he does it in so many ways. He takes members of his staff to conferences and training events to make them better. He sets aside time for individuals to personally mentor and coach them. He gives the people he leads freedom to risk and succeed and a safe place to fail and learn. He even adds value by paying his people well."

"But how has he added value to you personally?" I asked Dan.

"Where do I start?" exclaimed Dan. "I could give you a list." And he did:

Believing in me.

Speaking the truth in love to me.

Stretching me—way beyond my comfort zone but not outside of my gift zone.

Opening the world to me through foreign travel.

Modeling leadership in both the tough times and the fun times.

Speaking to others more highly of me than I deserve.

Opening doors in life that I could never have opened myself.

Consistently having my best interest at heart.

Allowing me into his inner circle.

Treating me like a younger brother—a gift of immeasurable value.

"If I had never met John, my whole life would be different—my career, my skills, my relationships," Dan explained. "He has added value to me every step of the way for two decades. How do you measure that?"

John never seems to miss an opportunity to add value to people. And that priority, as much as anything else, has made him a winner with people.

JOHN ... WITH A MAXWELL MENTORING MOMENT

At the core of my being, I believe that there is nothing in this life more important than people. Having embraced that truth, I try to live it out with integrity. To me that means doing everything in my power to add value to people.

If you desire to become a value adder, then take these things to heart:

VALUE PEOPLE

It all starts with your attitude toward people. Human relations expert Les Giblin remarked, "You can't make the other fellow feel important in your presence if you secretly feel that he is a nobody." Isn't that true? Don't you find it difficult to do something kind for people when you dislike them?

> "You can't make the other fellow feel important in your presence if you secretly feel that he is a nobody."
>
> —LES GIBLIN

The way we see people is often the difference between manipulating and motivating them. If we don't want to help people, yet we want them to help us, then we get in trouble. We manipulate people when we move them for our *personal* advantage. However, we motivate people when we move them for *mutual* advantage. Adding value to others is often a win-win proposition.

How do you see people? Are they potential recipients of value you can give, or do they tend to be nuisances along your path to success? Author Sydney J. Harris said, "People want to be appreciated, not impressed. They want to be regarded as human beings, not as sounding boards for other people's egos. They want to be treated as an end in themselves, not as a means towards the gratification of another's vanity." If you want to add value to people, you have to value them first.

MAKE YOURSELF MORE VALUABLE

We've talked about the phrase "you cannot give what you do not have." There are people who possess good hearts and the desire to give, yet they have very little to offer. Why? Because they have not first added value to themselves. Making yourself more valuable is not an entirely selfish act. When you acquire knowledge, learn a new skill, or gain experience, you not only improve yourself, but you also increase your ability to help others.

In 1974 I committed myself to the pursuit of personal growth. I knew that it would help me to be a better minister, so I began to continually read books, listen to tapes, attend conferences, and learn from better leaders. At the time, I had no idea that this commitment would be the most important thing I would ever do to help others. But that has turned out to be the case. As I improve myself, I am better able to help others improve. The more I grow, the more I can help others grow. The same will be true for you. If you want to add value to people, you must make yourself more valuable.

KNOW WHAT PEOPLE VALUE

Since you have read the chapters "Listen with Your Heart" and "Find the Keys to Their Hearts," you have a good grasp on the principle behind this practice. If you've already begun to practice it, then you know that it can be very time-consuming. But you also know it can be the most important step in adding value to others. Once we know what people value, with some effort we can add value to them.

I make it standard practice to note what the people in my life value from me, and you should too. Here are some examples from my own life:

Margaret, my wife, values my time with her, and my attention.

My children, Elizabeth and Joel Porter, value the legacy Margaret and I are leaving them.

Larry, my brother, values my prayers and our time together.

Eric and Troy, my nephews, value the fatherly advice and unconditional love I give them.

Linda, my assistant, values my time and effectiveness, because she is an integral part of it.

John, the president of my nonprofit organization, EQUIP, values the leadership and opportunities I give him.

Kirk, the president of my company ISS, values my friendship and partnership.

Tom values my friendship and mentoring.

Rick values my "big brother" relationship with him.

Joel values the networking opportunities I can give him.

I could go on, but I don't want to bore you. The point is that we must take the time to know what our most valuable people value.

By the way, adding value to others is not only a gift to them; it is a gift to you. The people I have just listed continually add value to my life. Some have given so much to me that no matter how much I do for them, I will never even the score.

LES . . . ON BRINGING IT HOME

Adding value to people is one of the reasons God put us here on earth. You cannot go wrong by helping others to live a better life or to reach their potential.

To apply John's teaching to your own life . . .

Forget about:
Trying to become a person of success, and instead become a person of value.

Ask:
Who adds value to my life, and to whom would I most like to add value?

Do it:
Make a list of the people in your life and note exactly what they value most from you.

Remember:
If you don't truly value the person, he or she will never feel important in your presence.

19

REMEMBER A
PERSON'S STORY

*Many a man would rather you heard his story
than granted his request.*
—PHILLIP STANHOPE, EARL OF CHESTERFIELD

LES . . . ON SEEING THE PRACTICE IN ACTION

"Les," John will say, "tell me about your dad. How are he and your mom doing since they moved to Phoenix?"

It's just like John to recall that my parents recently moved.

"And tell me about your brothers," he'll continue. "What's the latest with them?"

John always seems to remember my story—just as he does with so many people. He does it well, often, and consistently. When he has met people, I've heard him flat-out ask them to tell him their stories. So I asked him how he learned to be a collector of people's stories.

"To begin with, I love a good story—whether I'm learning about someone I've just met or hearing about an adventure from someone I've known my whole life. In fact, when I spend time with my dad, who is now eighty-two, our time is always filled with storytelling. We talk about the new things that are happening in our lives, but often the stories are ones I have heard dozens of times. Some Dad loves to tell over and over. Others I ask him to tell. Some I love retelling."

"But you seem to go out of your way to get the story of someone you just met," I commented.

"That's true. Whenever I have a few minutes with someone," John said, "I ask him to tell me his story, because I know that time in the conversation will focus entirely on him, his interests, dreams, uniqueness, disappointments, questions, hopes—his journey. While that person enjoys the personal attention, I gain insight into the keys to his life. Learning a person's story is a great way to connect with him. Remembering his journey and building on it is the greatest way to develop a strong relationship.

"Just the other day I took a taxi from the San Diego airport over to Coronado. And I talked to the cab driver," said John. "His name was Raphael. I asked him his story, and he told me that he had lived on Coronado thirty-five years, and there he had found something he'd not found anywhere else in his life: community. Every afternoon he meets his friends at a local market, where they talk and play games. He was so pleased that I asked and he was so delighted to tell his story that he invited me to the market."

That shows how great a connection you can make in a

short time by simply asking people to tell you their stories. And just imagine the impression it will make when you remember each story: it will help you to reconnect with people very quickly.

JOHN ... WITH A MAXWELL MENTORING MOMENT

There are so many good reasons to learn a person's story. Here are just a few that keep motivating me to continue this practice with others:

> *Requesting* a person's story says, "You could be special."
> *Remembering* a person's story says, "You are special."
> *Reminding* a person of his or her story says, "You are special to me."
> *Repeating* a person's story to others says, "You should be special to them."

The result? You become special to the person who shared a story with you.

There are really just three small steps when it comes to embracing this practice in order to win with people. The key is to cultivate the habit of actually taking these steps with the people in your life.

1. Ask

When you meet someone new, after the introductions and initial pleasantries, don't hesitate. Dive in and ask to hear the person's story. You can do it any number of ways: you can flat-out ask, "What's your story?" You can request that he tell you about himself. You can ask where he is from or how he got into the field he's in. Use your own style.

If you've never tried this kind of thing before and you worry that it might be awkward the first few times you do it, then practice with people you are unlikely to see again—the driver in a cab, a passenger on a plane, a waitress in a restaurant. Once you become comfortable asking questions of total strangers, the rest will be easy.

2. LISTEN

Years ago I came across a list of suggestions for good listening. (I think I clipped it from *Bits and Pieces*.) Here were some of the tips:

> Look the speaker in the eye.
>
> Be attentive—don't roll your eyes or grimace when you hear something you don't agree with.
>
> Don't interrupt—try phrases like "Go on" or "I see" instead of "Now, that reminds me . . ."
>
> Tell the speaker what you think you heard; begin by saying, "Let me see if I understand . . ."

The main idea is to really focus on the other person. The problem many people have is that while the other person speaks, they are thinking more about what they want to say when it's their turn instead of focusing on listening. When you give people your undivided attention, then you are in a better position to achieve the next step.

3. REMEMBER

Some people have a knack for numbers, others for names or faces. But just about everyone has the capacity to remember stories. Small children remember them. And stories have been recited and sung from memory for thousands of years. Even long stories, such as the Iliad and the Odyssey—believed to have been created nearly three thousand years ago—were sung for three centuries before being written down. Stories stay with us.

A couple of years ago, the conference department at Injoy received a letter from Ellis Brust, formerly of St. Michael and All Angels Episcopal Church, that tells the power of remembering a person's story. Here's what it said:

> One of my leaders in the church has just opened a franchise fast-food place in the small East Texas town of Gilmer. He is in business with two other men in the church and they are committed to running the business with sound Christian principles. I took him to hear John three or four years ago and he recalled John's Nordstrom's stories [about how their employees go the extra mile]. He has tried to train his employees using these principles.
>
> On the first week of operation, he overheard two little old ladies talking about the soft drink selection and one of them was disappointed that there was no Diet Dr. Pepper offered. He spoke with the woman who was diabetic and preferred Diet Dr. Pepper to other diet drinks. He got in his car, drove to the 7-11, purchased a six-pack of Diet Dr. Pepper, took the woman a cup of ice and a can of the drink. He told her that there would always be a case

of Diet Dr. Pepper in the refrigerator with her name on it, and she just needed to tell the person at the counter who she was and what her beverage preference was and she would get it.

The shocked woman said, "Young man, I have been in this town my whole life. I have many influential friends and they will all hear what you just did for me. Thank you, and we will be regular customers."

I thought you would want to know one small way your work is changing lives. Keep up the good work.

Was what the restaurant owner did a big deal? Did it change the lady's life? No. In fact, we don't know if he ever talked to her again or learned anything else about her story. But he made her feel special, and it served her well. If we care about people, really listen to them, and try to remember their stories, we can make an impact on them. And we can make them feel like a million bucks.

LES . . . ON BRINGING IT HOME

Researchers call it a "commitment script." It's part of a person's life narrative that is particularly meaningful and personal. From my own experience and from numerous studies, I can attest to the fact that when you tap into it with another person, when you take the time to explore it and remember it, you will make an extremely valuable connection.[1]

To apply John's teaching to your own life . . .

Forget about:

Telling your own story and listen to the story of others.

Ask:

What's your story?

Do it:

Bring up some aspect of a person's story the next time you see him or her.

Remember:

Everyone loves to tell his story.

20

TELL A GOOD STORY

The universe is made of stories, not atoms.
—MURIEL RUKEYSER

LES . . . ON SEEING THE PRACTICE IN ACTION

I spotted John on the curb at the Seattle airport and pulled up to get him. After tossing his bag into the back of my Jeep, I slid in behind the wheel. Then off we went to dinner at a hotel before a speaking engagement.

After a few minutes of catching up, we arrived at the hotel. As we walked through the lobby, John said, "Hold on a second. I want to tell you a story." He took me down a hallway, and we ducked into a meeting room.

"This place is very special to me," John explained. He pointed to a chair at the end of a conference table. "I was sitting in this chair right here when ISS evolved into the company it is today," John began, referencing one of his organizations. He pointed to each chair and explained who had been seated in it. Then he laid out the entire process of what happened that day: how he had flown to Seattle to get advice from a business executive; how his dream to help pastors raise money to expand their churches crossed over from vision to reality that day; how he recruited that business leader to assist churches on a national level.

The way John told it, I could easily visualize the whole thing and feel his enthusiasm. "I tell you, Les, coming back to a place where something good happened always renews my gratitude."

The lesson of this story stuck. John told me that story eight years ago, and I still remember it vividly. In fact, I can't help but think of it every time I drive by that hotel. It was an important point of connection to John for me at the time. He included me in a private part of his life—sharing his heart, his dreams, and his personal history. It made me feel good—and still does.

As a communicator, I'm always watching to see how people speak to an audience. John always tells a good story—in front of an audience as well as one-on-one. And he uses lots of stories when he communicates. So I asked him why.

"That's easy: stories stick; principles fade," said John. "If you want people to remember what you said, tell a story.

"Let me tell you something else," he continued. "It took a while for me to learn the lesson about stories in my writing. I'm so bottom-line that I used to just teach principles without many stories. But a friend convinced me to change my style. And it's made a big difference for my readers. As a writer, you've got to ask yourself, 'Will the reader turn the page?' The person most likely will if I am telling a good story."

I haven't met a person yet who doesn't love a good story. That's one of the reasons storytellers are so magnetic!

JOHN ... WITH A MAXWELL MENTORING MOMENT

In the fall of 1999, Margaret, some friends, and I visited the small town of Jonesborough, Tennessee. More than seven thousand people from all over the country, many at considerable expense, came there to sit for hours on end on blankets, on folding chairs, sometimes even in the rain. Why? They wanted to attend the annual National Storytelling Festival.

We watched one storyteller after another captivate listeners. The stories were diverse—sad, happy, funny, sentimental, historical, fictitious, mythical. Some had a great message; others simply entertained. But all the stories and storytellers had one thing in common: they had the power to captivate their listeners.

At the end of the conference, my friends and I discussed why these storytellers were so effective. "What traits did they have that made them so successful?" we asked. Here's the list we came up with:

Enthusiasm—They enjoyed what they were doing and expressed themselves with joy and vitality.

Animation—The presentations were marked by lively facial expressions and gestures.

Audience participation—Nearly every storyteller involved the audience in some way, asking listeners to sing, clap, repeat phrases, or do sign language.

Spontaneity—The storytellers responded freely to their listeners.

Memorization—Telling their stories without notes allowed for eye contact.

Humor—Humor was interjected in both serious and sad stories.

Creativity—Classic themes were told from a fresh perspective.

Personal—Most stories were told in the first person.

Heartwarming—Their stories made people feel good for having heard them.

Storytelling is very effective one-on-one, in small group conversation, and in front of large audiences. Invariably, the person who tells the best stories becomes the one to whom others turn their attention.

Storytelling is a skill that comes with practice, and anyone can learn to develop it. If you don't have much experience with it, or you would like to improve, then allow me to give you a few tips:

SHARE SOMETHING YOU'VE EXPERIENCED

The stories we tell the best are the ones we've lived. We care about them, we know the material, and we know how they have affected us. And we can shape and embellish them any way we want. Everybody has had experiences that others would be interested in.

> The stories we tell the best are the ones we've lived.

TELL IT WITH THE GOAL OF CONNECTING

The people who have the toughest time telling stories are the ones who try to impress others with them. If that describes you, then change your goal. Tell stories with the purpose of connecting with others. Put the focus on the listener, and your storytelling skills will improve overnight.

PUT YOUR HEART INTO IT

People love humor, but not everyone can tell a funny story. If you can, go with it. But never underestimate the power of a story from the heart. (If you want evidence, look at the sales figures of the *Chicken Soup for the Soul* books!) If you want to tell a connecting story, make it warm. Put your heart into it. And don't be afraid to show people that you care about what you're talking about.

ASSUME THAT OTHERS WANT TO HEAR IT

One of the biggest mistakes novice storytellers make is being tentative. Nothing makes a story go flat more quickly than a timid delivery. If you're going to tell a story, be bold. Be energetic. Be engaging. Go for it, or don't go at all.

I've read that the "elite" often criticized President Lincoln for telling too many stories. But he didn't let it stop him, because he knew what worked with people. He remarked, "They say I tell a great many stories; I reckon I do, but I have found in the course of a long experience that common people, take them as they run, are more easily informed through the medium of a broad illustration than in any other way, and as to what the hypercritical few may think, I don't care."

Follow the lead of Lincoln and other great leaders who knew how to win with people. Tell a good story, engage them at the heart level, and win them over.

LES ... ON BRINGING IT HOME

Research supports the value of being able to relate your thoughts and ideas through stories. In fact, one recent study revealed that those who use storytelling as a means of relating to others engender greater authenticity and self-esteem. It turns out their self-expression makes others feel good, and they feel better about themselves in the process.[1]

To apply John's teaching to your own life ...

Forget about:

Being a professional storyteller.

Ask:

How can I make my point come through stronger with a story?

Do it:

Tell a story instead of relaying only facts.

Remember:

Stories stick—principles fade.

21

GIVE WITH NO
STRINGS ATTACHED

Life's most persistent and urgent question is:
What are you doing for others?
—MARTIN LUTHER KING, JR.

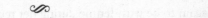

LES ... ON SEEING THE PRACTICE IN ACTION

Whenever I visit John at his office in Atlanta, one of the
people I always see is Linda Eggers, John's assistant. On a
recent trip as I chatted with her, I began querying her for stories to illustrate the idea of giving with no strings attached.

"Who's got a good story?" I asked. "Who should I go
talk to?"

"How about me?" Linda responded. She began telling me
one story after another, but one in particular seemed to mean
the most to her. It occurred when her youngest daughter,
Kim, was getting ready to graduate from high school. It was

an especially hectic time at the office too. And Linda's middle child, Jennie, who was living in California, had recently given birth under difficult circumstances.

The day before Kim's graduation, Linda got word that Jenny was having serious complications that would require surgery.

"I'm a very steady person," said Linda. "There aren't too many things that can get to me. But I was totally overwhelmed by the situation."

Linda said that when she sat down and told John about all that was happening, after some kind words and prayer, John offered to step in and help her. The first thing he did was buy her a ticket so that she could be with Jennie that day for the surgery—a ticket with a return flight on the red-eye so that Linda could get back for Kim's graduation. And he bought her another ticket so that Linda could go back out again to be with Jennie during her recovery.

"How many employers do you know who would do something like that?" said Linda. "Because of his busy schedule, it was a real inconvenience for John to lose me during that time. But he just said, 'You take whatever time you need and do what needs to be done,' and he really meant it. I was gone for another whole week."

Linda's wasn't the only story I heard. Charlie Wetzel, John's writer for more than a decade, told me about the time John offered to send him to a weeklong writer's conference after he had worked for John only a year. When Charlie explained that he couldn't go because it was his first wedding anniversary, John offered to send Charlie and his wife. And more than one person told about a time when they were barely making it financially and John slipped them money so that they could go out for a nice dinner with their spouse.

Generosity is an extremely appealing quality. When someone gives to others—with no strings attached—it really makes them feel special.

JOHN . . . WITH A MAXWELL MENTORING MOMENT

Jesuit theologian Pierre Teilhard de Chardin said, "The most satisfying thing in life is to have been able to give a large part of one's self to others." Anyone who has unselfishly helped another person knows this to be true. Yet not everyone is able to adopt an ongoing mind-set of giving toward others. Why is that? First of all, I believe it has nothing to do with circumstances. I've met generous people with almost nothing who were willing to share what little they possessed. And I've met well-off people who were stingy with their time, money, and talents.

The issue is really attitude. I've found that people who enjoy giving with no strings attached usually exhibit two characteristics that anyone can embrace:

1. THEY HAVE AN ABUNDANCE MENTALITY

If you've read Stephen Covey's book *The Seven Habits of Highly Effective People* (Free Press, 1989), then you are familiar with the concepts related to scarcity and abundance mind-sets. In a nutshell, people with a scarcity mind-set believe that in life, there's only a limited supply of anything to go around, whether it's money, resources, opportunity, and so forth. They see the world as a pie with a limited number of slices. Once they're gone, they're gone. As a result, they fight to get their piece—and once they have it, they protect it.

People possessing an abundance mind-set believe that there is plenty of everything to go around. If life is a pie, and others are helping themselves to pieces, the solution of the person with the abundance mind-set is to bake another pie. There is always more money to be made, more (or different) resources to be discovered, additional opportunities to be pursued. An old solution isn't working anymore? Don't worry: someone will find a new one. The inventors, entrepreneurs, and explorers of the world are continually creating new "pies" so that everyone can get a slice.

My own take on this is that people tend to fall into one of two categories: they are either takers or makers. Takers are people who take, grab, and consume whatever they can to meet their own needs. They see life as a rat race. Of course, the main problem with that is that even if you win, you're still a rat. Makers, on the other hand, are people who give, create, and make things happen. They create progress and foster success for others. They are just as likely to give as to take because they are continually helping to create more for everyone.

People who habitually give with no strings attached almost always have an abundance mentality. They are generous because they believe that if they give, they will not run out of

> "When we refrain from giving, with a scarcity mentality, the little we have will become less. When we give generously, with an abundance mentality, what we give away will multiply."
>
> —HENRI NOUWEN

resources. Pastor and former college professor Henri Nouwen states, "When we refrain from giving, with a scarcity mentality, the little we have will become less. When we give generously, with an abundance mentality, what we give away will multiply."

I have found this to be true. Someone once asked me why he should adopt an abundance mentality, and he was surprised by my answer. I told him that if you believe in abundance, that's what life gives you. If you believe in scarcity, then that's what you get. I don't know why that is, but after fifty years of paying attention to people's attitudes and watching how life unfolded for them, I know it to be true. So if you desire to be more generous, change your thinking and your attitude when it comes to abundance. Not only will it allow you to be more generous, but also it will change your life.

2. They See the Big Picture

People who give with no strings attached are usually aware of the help *they* have received along the way. They recognize that they are standing on the shoulders of previous generations. The progress they make is due, at least in part, to the work and sacrifice of those who have gone before them. Because of this, they are determined to do for the next generation what was done for them.

I came across a poem by W. A. Dromgoale called "The Bridge Builder." It beautifully illustrates this desire to give to others:

> An old man walking a lonesome road,
> Came at the evening, cold and gray,
> To a chasm vast and wide and deep.

The old man crossed in the twilight dim,
The rolling stream had no fears for him;
But he turned when safe on the other side,
And built a bridge to span the tide.

"Old man," said a fellow traveler near,
"You are wasting your strength with building here,
Your journey will end with the passing day,
You never again will pass this way.
You've crossed the chasm, deep and wide,
Why build you this bridge at eventide?"

The builder lifted his old gray head,
"Good friend, in the path I have come," he said,
"There followeth after me today,
A youth whose feet must pass this way.
The chasm that was nought to me,
To the fair headed youth may a pitfall be.
He too must cross in the twilight dim—
Good friend, I am building this bridge for him."[1]

To become better givers, we need greater perspective.
When we realize how much we have benefited from the kind-
ness of others, it becomes much easier for us to be generous.
And one of the best things is that giving is so rewarding.
College president and educational reformer Horace Mann
commented, "We must be purposely kind and generous or we
miss the best part of existence. The heart that goes out of
itself gets large and full of joy. This is the great secret of the

inner life. We do ourselves the most good doing something for others." When we give unselfishly, we will gain something in return.

LES ... ON BRINGING IT HOME

This lesson certainly rings true in my therapy sessions with clients. And it's backed up by plenty of research. Studies have shown that the higher one's level of helpfulness to others, the greater well-being one will experience. Researchers call it "generativity," and it is consistently linked to greater personal growth and even physical health.[2]

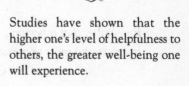

Studies have shown that the higher one's level of helpfulness to others, the greater well-being one will experience.

To apply John's teaching to your own life ...

Forget about:

Scarcity; instead, focus on abundance.

Ask:

Whom can I help that will give nothing in return?

Do it:

Be purposely kind and generous to a specific person.

Remember:

You do yourself the most good when you are doing something good for others.

22

LEARN YOUR
MAILMAN'S NAME

*Remember that a person's name is to that person the
sweetest and most important sound in any language.*
—DALE CARNEGIE

LES . . . ON SEEING THE PRACTICE IN ACTION

John tells the story about how he used to memorize the
names of people who attended his church when he was the
senior pastor of Skyline Wesleyan Church in San Diego,
California. He used to make an offer to visitors: if they would
allow someone to take their pictures on Sunday after the
service, John promised to learn their names by the following
Sunday. John did that until he finished his tenure at the
church in 1995. Fulfilling that promise, John was able to
memorize the names of more than twenty-two hundred
people and greet them by name.

In the summer of 2004, Skyline Church celebrated its fiftieth anniversary, and John and Margaret were delighted to return and be a part of the celebration. John told me that thousands of people attended, many of whom he had not seen in nine years. He was thankful that each person had a name tag. "But as I approached one couple," John told me, "the husband covered his name tag. When I called him by name he laughed and said, 'I was just checking to see if you could still remember names.'"

"That doesn't surprise me," I said, "but it still impresses me."

"You know," John replied, "at fifty-seven, it's not as easy as it once was, but I still work at remembering names."

I've long admired this skill and personal approach of John's. In fact, it inspired me in my work as a professor to learn the names of several hundred students in my classes each semester at the university. Why do we do it? Because we know that a person's name is his personal signboard to the world, his most intimate, distinctive possession. And when you remember a person's name, it can make him or her feel like a million bucks.

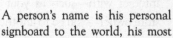

A person's name is his personal signboard to the world, his most intimate, distinctive possession.

JOHN ... WITH A MAXWELL
MENTORING MOMENT

In 1937 the granddaddy of all people-skills books was published. It was an overnight hit, eventually selling more than fifteen million copies. That book was *How to Win Friends and*

Influence People (Simon & Schuster, 1981), by Dale Carnegie. What made that book so valuable was Carnegie's understanding of human nature. I love his simple words of wisdom. Something that I learned early from Carnegie was this: remember and use a person's name. "We should be aware of the *magic* contained in a name . . . The name sets the individual apart; it makes him or her unique among all others. The information we are imparting or the request we are making takes on a special importance when we approach the situation with the name of the individual. From the waitress to the senior executive, the name will work magic as we deal with others."

What was true in 1937 is even more applicable in our fast-paced world. These days an account number or a title too often replaces a person's name. Remembering names can help enhance your personal image, improve your style, and, most importantly, increase your impact on others. And when you take the time to learn the names of not only your clients and important acquaintances, but also the everyday people you interact with—such as your postal worker or neighborhood store owner—you go to another level of relational connectivity.

If you desire to improve your skill with names, here are a few suggestions:

RECOGNIZE THE VALUE OF A NAME

How do you feel when someone calls you by the wrong name? How about when you kindly correct the person and spend time with him, and he still gets your name wrong? How about when people haven't seen you for a long time, and they still remember your name? Doesn't it make you feel good? (And doesn't it also impress you?) When people care enough to know your name, they make you feel valued.

Playwright William Shakespeare wrote, "Good name, in man or woman, is the immediate jewel of their souls.—Who steals my purse steals trash; but he that filches from me my good name, robs me of that which not enriches him, and makes me poor indeed."[1]

USE THE SAVE METHOD

My friend Jerry Lucas is known as "Dr. Memory." He has spent the years following his hugely successful run in the NBA helping schoolchildren and adults improve their memories through a variety of innovative techniques. One of the things he teaches is called the SAVE Method. Here's how it works:

S—Say the name three times in conversation.

A—Ask a question about the name (for example, how it is spelled) or about the person.

V—Visualize the person's prominent physical or person- ality feature.

E—End the conversation with the name.

Years ago Jerry showed how useful his method could be by remembering the names of every guest in the audience at the *Tonight Show*. I believe it can also help you remember the first and last names of the people you meet.

IN CASE OF MEMORY FAILURE . . .

Almost everyone has trouble recalling names on some occasions. When this happens, try to recall the situation in which you met the person or last saw him or her. If you can't recall even that, then ask, "How long has it been?" Perhaps that will jog your memory.

If you're meeting people along with a friend or colleague, sometimes you can help each other out. Introduce the person whose name you do remember to the person whose name you don't, and perhaps the individual will volunteer his name. Or you can agree with your friend ahead of time to come to each other's aid. My wife and I do this. When we make introductions, Margaret knows that if I don't introduce someone by name, I'm not sure I remember it correctly. And she will quickly introduce herself and get the other person's name in return.

When all else fails, just say, "I'm so sorry; I remember you well, but I'm afraid your name has slipped my mind." Then after the individual reminds you, use the SAVE method so that you are less likely to forget it again in the future.

GO EASY ON YOURSELF IF YOU FORGET

If you work at it, you *will* become better at remembering people's names. Don't be too hard on yourself, however, when you blow it. That's what I did recently when meeting a couple whose last name was Lake. One of the things I do when learning a name is to link the name to a mental image. When I was introduced to the Lakes, I immediately placed a mental image of a lake on their heads and thought of Hargus Lake where I grew up. A few days later when I saw them again, I mistakenly asked, "How are you doing tonight, Mr. and Mrs. Hargus?" Sometimes even our best practices fail us!

LES . . . ON BRINGING IT HOME

One hardly needs a research study to validate the points John is making about the value of remembering people's names. However, if you want to know whether it is substantiated by studies, I could point you to a mountain of research that shows exactly how a person's mood and self-evaluation are consistently improved when another person remembers him or her personally.[2] There is simply no question of the value of remembering people's names.

To apply John's teaching to your own life . . .

Forget about:

Blaming your "bad" memory and exert some effort to remember people's names.

Ask:

What can you tell me about the origin of your name or how it's spelled?

Do it:

Use the SAVE Method with each new person you meet this week.

Remember:

A person's name is one of his or her most valuable possessions.

23

POINT OUT PEOPLE'S STRENGTHS

*The praises of others may be of use in teaching us,
not what we are, but what we ought to be.*
—AUGUST W. HARE

LES . . . ON SEEING THE PRACTICE IN ACTION

I am constantly amazed by the number of high-caliber people John has on his staff. He seems to be surrounded by all-stars. When asked about his secret, he responded, "Two things. First, I try to hire the best leaders I can find. If I can hire a few '9s' and '10s,' then they will attract and hire '8s' and '9s.' Second, I always try to put people in their areas of strength."

"Okay," I said, "let me quiz you on some of the people in your circle. I'll give you a name, and you tell me their strength."

"Okay, shoot," John answered.

"Tim Elmore."

"There's nobody better than Tim at examining a passage of Scripture, searching it thoroughly, and pulling out teaching points from it."

"Linda Eggers."

"Linda's attention to detail is off the charts; she runs my whole life. But I'd have to say that her greatest strength is the confidence she instills in others. When someone talks to Linda, they feel that they've talked to me."

"Dan Reiland."

"Dan's greatest skill is leading and developing leaders on his staff. You know, back at Skyline he was my executive pastor; he led the staff and ran the church day to day while I traveled nationally."

"Did Dan come to you with experience as an executive pastor?" I asked.

"No, no, when I met Dan, he was an intern," John explained. "He had worked briefly as a youth pastor, and when he started working for me as a regular employee after seminary, I put him in charge of children's education. But over the years, he did a lot of different things. Anytime I wanted to start a new ministry, Dan was my man.

"As we worked together, a pattern of strength emerged. Dan always had the big picture, championed the vision, and possessed influence with his peers and volunteers. And he had a particular knack for developing people. As those strengths emerged, it became obvious that he was the right person to become my executive pastor."

Jim Collins, in his book *Good to Great* (Harperbusiness,

2001), writes about the concept of getting the right people on the bus and then making sure each is in the right seat. That's essentially what John was saying. When you look for and point out people's strengths, then you are able to help people take the place that's best for them and the organization. And that helps everyone win!

JOHN ... WITH A MAXWELL MENTORING MOMENT

People often make a mistake in their personal development when they focus too much on their weaknesses. As a result, they spend all their time trying to shore up those weaknesses instead of maximizing the strengths they possess. Similarly, it's a mistake to focus on the weaknesses of others. The self-proclaimed "experts" who spend their time telling others what's wrong with them *never* win with people. Most people simply avoid them.

Instead, we need to focus on finding people's strengths and pointing them out. Here's why:

POINTING OUT STRENGTHS UNDERLINES PEOPLE'S UNIQUENESS

Most people have strengths that they rarely get to use. Those strengths may be job skills, knowledge, general abilities, personality characteristics, or other attributes. I once read an interesting fact based on research, saying that every person can do at least one thing better than ten thousand other people. Think about that! You possess an ability that can't be matched by anyone in your town or neighborhood . . . or in your college or university . . . or in your company or maybe even in your industry.

Have you discovered that ability? If so, you are probably well on your way to pursuing your life's purpose. If you haven't, wouldn't you love it if someone came alongside you and pointed it out? How would you feel about that person? I bet you'd be pretty grateful.

Why not try to become that kind of person in someone else's life? When you do, you just might be helping others to discover the thing God created them to do.

PEOPLE ARE MOTIVATED IN THEIR AREAS OF STRENGTH

I once read that a survey was taken of workers across the United States in which it was found that nearly 85 percent of those interviewed said that they could work harder on the job. More than half of them claimed they could double their effectiveness if they wanted to. Why would that be? It is because so few people are working in their areas of strength. Do you get excited when asked to work in an area of weakness? I certainly don't.

Marcus Buckingham and Donald O. Clifton have done tremendous research in this area. If you want to learn more, I suggest you read their book: *Now, Discover Your Strengths* (Free Press, 2001). But know this: when you work in your areas of strength, you don't need much external motivation. If people have been grinding away at tasks in their weak areas, and they are reassigned to work in areas of strength, watch their motivation, enthusiasm, and productivity skyrocket.

PEOPLE ADD THE MOST VALUE IN THEIR STRENGTH ZONES

People often ask me what the key to my success is. And I tell them that I think it can be attributed to three things:

(1) the goodness of God; (2) the excellent people around me; and (3) my ability to stay in my strength zone. It took the first five years of my professional life to figure out what my strengths were. But with the passing of years since then, I've narrowed my focus down to fewer and fewer things.

The Law of the Niche in my book *The 17 Indisputable Laws for Teamwork* states, "All players have a place where they add the most value." That place is their "strength zone." I'm worthless at most things. But I do four things really well: lead, create, communicate, and network. And as much as possible, I stick to those things.

As a leader and employer, I try to help others do the same. I help them find their strength zones, and I try to position them there as much as possible. You see, a successful person finds the right place for himself. But a successful leader finds the right place for others. How do I do that?

A successful person finds the right place for himself. But a successful leader finds the right place for others.

First, I look for the best in others. Anybody can see weaknesses, mistakes, and shortcomings in others. That's no unique skill. Seeing only the good things is harder. Hall of Fame baseball player Reggie Jackson said that the best major-league baseball leaders possess that ability. He observed, "A great manager has a knack for making ballplayers think they are better than they think they are. He forces you to have a good opinion of yourself. He lets you know he believes in you. He makes you get more out of yourself. And once you learn how good you really are, you never settle for playing anything less than your very best." That's true in any area of life: business, parenting, marriage, ministry, and so forth. Don't look for the flaws, warts, and blemishes in others. Look for their best.

Second, I speak up. You can think the world of others, but if you never actually tell them, then you don't really help them. I have always believed that all people have a "success seed" within them. Most never find it and therefore fail to reach their potential. I often look at other people and ask, "What are their success seeds?" When I discover them, I point them out to those individuals. Then I fertilize those seeds with encouragement and water them with opportunity.

LES . . . ON BRINGING IT HOME

One of the most cutting-edge aspects of contemporary research in psychology has to do with what are termed "signature strengths." Everyone has a number of positive qualities that represent his or her strengths, but some of those are more important and more central to a person's identity. When you can point them out to others, research shows, a person is far more likely to use them, to put them on display, and to embrace them as a key component of his or her identity.

To apply John's teaching to your own life . . .

Forget about:

The weaknesses of others.

Ask:

What does this individual do exceptionally well?

Do it:

Every day this week, tell at least one person what strength you see in him or her.

Remember:

Every person in the world possesses the seeds for success.

24

WRITE NOTES OF ENCOURAGEMENT

*The power of words is immense. A well-chosen word
has often sufficed to stop a flying army, to change
defeat into victory, and to save an empire.*
—EMILE DE GIRARDIN

LES . . . ON SEEING THE PRACTICE IN ACTION

I always love to see the inner sanctums of great leaders. You can learn much about people when you see where they work. Recently I was in John's home office, where he does most of his thinking, dreaming, writing, and creating. Among the memorabilia that is important to him, one cannot help but notice an impressive collection of John Wesley's works. In fact, it may be one of the most extensive privately held historical collections of its kind. And as a student of Wesley myself, I was intrigued.

"What's your most prized piece in this collection, John?" I asked, pointing to a shelf of antique books.

"It would have to be a letter I have that was signed by John Wesley and postscripted by his brother Charles," John said as he took me around the corner to see it hanging in a frame on the wall.

"Is it an important letter?" I asked, trying to decipher Wesley's spidery handwriting.

"It's a letter to a friend, giving him parenting advice. I prize it because it is written in Wesley's hand and signed by him," John said. "But if you want to talk about *important* letters by Wesley, then you have to consider the letter he wrote to William Wilberforce.

"In 1791, William Wilberforce was facing one more discouraging defeat in his attempt to abolish Britain's slave trade," explained John. "Then he received a letter from John Wesley. That now-famous letter would prove to be a continuing source of strength for the rest of his life."

John went quickly into his files under the topic of "encouragement" and found the text of that Wesley letter and read it aloud to me:

London, February 26, 1791

Dear Sir:

Unless the divine power has raised you up . . . I see not how you can go through your glorious enterprise, in opposing that execrable villainy, which is the scandal of religion, of England, and of human nature. Unless God has raised you up for this very thing, you will be worn out by the opposition of men and devils. But, "if God be for you, who can be against you?" Are all of them stronger than God? O "be not weary in well doing!" Go on, in the name of God and in the power of His might, till even American slavery (the vilest that ever saw the sun) shall vanish away before it.

. . . That He who has guided you from your youth up, may continue to strengthen you in this and all things, is the prayer of,

Your affectionate servant,
J. Wesley

"Four days after writing that letter," John recounted, "Wesley was dead. And once again Wilberforce was defeated when the vote was taken in Parliament. Ultimately Wilberforce prevailed, but in the intervening years, he was vilified and faced so many disappointments. His opponents even arranged for him to be challenged to a duel and made an attempt to kill him."

John continued, "He was tempted to give up the fight more than once. But every time he became discouraged, he returned to Wesley's letter. Each time he read it, it was like the first time. It never failed to encourage and strengthen him.

"If you don't believe in the encouraging power of the written note after hearing about that," John said, "you probably never will."

I can attest to the fact that John believes in that power. I've received several notes of encouragement from him over the years, and I still have many of them. They may not hold the historical value of Wesley's note to Wilberforce, but their value to me is priceless.

JOHN ... WITH A MAXWELL
MENTORING MOMENT

If you haven't already guessed it, I'm a real history buff. Let me tell you the rest of the story: in 1806, after working tirelessly for twenty years, Wilberforce finally succeeded in getting a bill passed that abolished the slave trade. Twenty-eight years later, on July 31, 1834, slavery itself was outlawed throughout the British Empire, freeing approximately 800,000 slaves. Although he did not live to see the realization of his dream, having died on August 5, 1833, no one was more responsible than William Wilberforce for the demise of slavery in the British Empire.

Wilberforce died one of the most esteemed men of his day and was buried in Westminster Abbey. His epitaph reads in part:

Eminent as he was in every department of public labour,
   And a leader in every work of charity,
Whether to relieve the temporal or the spiritual wants
   of his fellow men
His name will ever be specially identified
   With those exertions
Which, by the blessing of God, removed from England
   The guilt of the African slave trade,
And prepared the way for the abolition of slavery
   in every colony of the Empire.

Wilberforce had devoted his entire life and political career to a great cause: ending slavery. Yet he might not have prevailed had it not been for the encouraging note of John Wesley.

I have believed in the power of written notes of encouragement for many years—beginning before I received the Wesley letter as a gift from the people of Skyline Church after serving as their pastor. In fact, it was while leading Skyline that I asked my staff members to devote time every Monday to handwriting notes to people.

Written notes don't have to come from someone famous to be encouraging. A kind word given from the heart is always well received. If you've never mastered the practice of sending handwritten notes to people, then I want to encourage you to try this often neglected way of winning with people. Here's why:

ENCOURAGING NOTES HAVE A PERSONAL TOUCH

Today we communicate by telephone, digital pager, cell phone, fax machine, e-mail, and the Internet. In the hectic pace of our busy lives, who has time to correspond the old-fashioned way? Yet the more convenient our communication becomes, the more temporary it is. We forget how meaningful that personal touch can be. Few things beat opening a mailbox and pulling out a real note written by a real person. When you see the thoughts of someone you respect written in his or her own hand, it really means something.

Six days a week, regular mail service is provided by the United States Postal Service. Annually postal workers handle 170 billion pieces of mail. Yet, in this huge sea of mail, officials say personal letters account for less than 4 percent of the total. So on average, you will have to wade through twenty-five pieces of mail before you put your hands on one that contains a personal word. More than ever in this day and age, a handwritten note communicates that you care.

NOTES REPRESENT AN INVESTMENT BY THE WRITER

In his book *The Power of Encouragement* (Multnomah, 1997), my friend David Jeremiah says, "Written encouragement comes directly from the heart, uninterrupted and uninhibited. That's why it's so powerful." Haven't you known that to be true?

> "Written encouragement comes directly from the heart, uninterrupted and uninhibited. That's why it's so powerful."
>
> —DAVID JEREMIAH

Nineteenth-century writer Walt Whitman struggled for years to get anyone interested in his poetry. He became very discouraged. Then he received a note that read: "Dear sir, I am not blind to the worth of the wonderful gift of *Leaves of Grass*. I find it the most extraordinary piece of wit and wisdom that America has yet contributed. I greet you at the beginning of a great career." It was signed by Ralph Waldo Emerson.

I can't help but wonder what might have happened to Whitman had Emerson not invested in him by writing those kind words. That note was like fresh air to Whitman, who breathed in that encouragement and was inspired to keep writing. But you don't have to be a professional writer to make a difference in someone's life. Just taking the time to write is evidence of your willingness to invest in that person.

NOTES ARE REMEMBERED LONG AFTER THE WRITER HAS
FORGOTTEN THEM

For years I have made it a practice to write personal notes
to others. I often forget what I have written, but occasionally
someone who has received a note from me will show it to me
and tell me what an encouragement it was. It is in those
moments that I am reminded of the sustained and repeated
encouragement people receive from the written word.

You never can tell when something you write to others
will light them up in down times or sustain them when life
gets difficult. In the first *Chicken Soup for the Soul* (Health
Communications, 1993) book, teacher Sister Helen Mrosla
recounted how a spur-of-the-moment assignment in class
became a source of encouragement for her students. On a day
when her junior high math students were especially ornery,
she asked them to write down what they liked about each of
their fellow students. She then compiled the results over the
weekend and handed out the lists on the following Monday.

Years later when one of those students, Mark, was killed
in Vietnam, she and some of those former students got
together for the funeral. Afterward, Mark's father told the
group, "They found this on Mark when he was killed," and he
showed them a folded, refolded, and taped paper—the one he
had received years before from his teacher. Right after that,
Charlie, one of Mark's classmates, said, "I keep my list in my
desk drawer." Chuck's wife said, "Chuck put his in our wedding album." "I have mine, too," Marilyn said, "in my diary."

Standing there, Vicky reached into her pocketbook and
brought out her frazzled list, showing it to her teacher and
former classmates. Each person cherished the kind words of

encouragement they had received. That's the power of a few kind words.

LES . . . ON BRINGING IT HOME

You may be reluctant to take time writing notes to others because you believe that complimenting people verbally is enough. If so, you may be surprised by recent research into the topic of authenticity, which found that when a word of encouragement is written down for another person, it is often perceived to be more genuine than when it is spoken.[1] That leaves little doubt about the value of writing notes of encouragement to others.

> When a word of encouragement is written down for another person, it is often perceived to be more genuine than when it is spoken.

To apply John's teaching to your own life . . .

Forget about:
Being a perfect writer and focus on writing from the heart.

Ask:
What can I say that will be an encouragement now, as well as someday in the future?

Do it:
Take one hour today to write several notes to people for the sole purpose of encouraging them.

Remember:

Words have the power to give encouragement long after the writer has forgotten them.

25

HELP PEOPLE WIN

*The most important measure of how good
a game I played was how much better
I'd make my teammates play.*
—BILL RUSSELL, WINNER OF MORE NBA CHAMPIONSHIPS
THAN ANY OTHER PLAYER

LES ... ON SEEING THE PRACTICE IN ACTION

If I've ever met anyone who loves to see people win, it's John
Maxwell. That's the reason he writes books and leads seminars
and conferences. He believes he has something to offer to others to help them succeed. But John also helps people win on a
smaller scale, whether it's teaching his daughter how to sell
candy door-to-door for school when she was little, taking time
to give a struggling pastor advice to help him through a tough
time, or giving a young person with potential tremendous
responsibility. John loves to win, and he enjoys seeing others
win even more.

For many years, John did a one-day seminar that taught pastors and their church members how to partner in volunteer ministry. At the end of the session, he used to tell one of my favorite stories. It really typifies John's attitude toward helping others.

When John's nephew, Eric, was seven years old, he got ready to play his first game in his first season of Little League baseball. John and Margaret went to see the game, and of course, John wanted to help Eric win. Here's the story as John often tells it:

You've got to understand, Eric had never played baseball before. He's intimidated, he's scared, he's fearful, he's frightened. And his coach thinks it's the World Series! So Eric walks up to the plate. His helmet is way down over his ears, his uniform is way too big for him, and he can hardly hold the bat. He's petrified. So there he stands, facing the other team's pitcher, who is always the biggest kid. His name is Butch; he's got a big wad of bubble gum in his jaw, and peach fuzz all over his face.

Eric just kind of hugged the bat and closed his eyes and prayed. And that ball went whoosh! Strike one. Whoosh! Strike two. Whoosh! Strike three. I mean, just like that; and when the umpire said, "You're out," Eric just looked glad to be alive.

As he walked back to the dugout, parents started yelling at him and the coach was hollering at him. And I'm sitting there thinking, *This is my nephew, and he's scared*. So I went down to that little fence where Eric was, and I said, "Sweetheart, I don't know what they've told you about baseball, but let your Uncle John teach you something. Baseball is a very simple game."

He said, "What do you mean?"

I said, "You only have to do one thing. The next time you go up to bat, every time Butch throws the ball, you just swing the bat. That's all you have to do. Butch throws the ball; you swing the bat. Butch throws the ball; you swing the bat."

He looked at me and said, "That's all I gotta do?"

I said, "That's all. Don't worry about hitting that ball; just swing the bat." And all of a sudden a smile broke out on his face, and he said, "I can do that."

I said, "Sure you can do that! Go get 'em, boy."

The next time Eric got up to bat, Butch threw the ball and Eric swung the bat. He missed it by a mile. In fact, he swung so late the ball was already in the catcher's glove. I am now beginning to clap my hands. I am saying, "Wonderful swing, Eric, wonderful swing. That-a-boy! Every time Butch throws the ball, you swing the bat."

Butch throws the ball; Eric swings the bat. Butch throws the ball; he's missing it by about three feet. Finally, he strikes out on the third strike. I'm on my feet shouting, "Eric McCullogh, that is the finest strikeout I have ever seen in my life. Way to go!"

At that point, the coach looks up into the bleachers and gives me a dirty look. And the parents aren't too happy either. Margaret says, "Sweetheart, I'm gonna go to the car and read a book." But I don't care, because after this at bat, Eric is smiling.

Now, to be honest, I didn't think Eric was going to get

a hit that day. Besides, in Little League baseball, there's no such thing as a hit. If there's any kind of contact, it's not the bat hitting the ball; it's the ball hitting the bat. And if there's one thing I know, it's this: if the ball hits the bat, it doesn't have to go far; it just has to go fair. And in Little League baseball, if the ball goes anywhere in fair territory, you never stop running.

Well, I didn't think it was gonna happen, but it did. The third time up, Butch threw the ball; Eric swings; the ball hits the bat. It wasn't a crack out into center field; it was a thud. As soon as I saw the ball was fair, I'm out of the bleachers and I'm running down the first base line, saying, "Eric, keep on running, keep on running!"

As Eric goes around first base, I cut across the infield as fast as I can. I'm now at third base and I'm saying, "Come on, Eric! Come on, Eric!" Eric rounds third base, and together we slide safe into home. Eric gets up and brushes off his uniform, I get up and brush off my suit; and as we walked off the field, I just looked at the coach and gave him a smile.

We went home that day to Eric's house. His parents had to work and didn't get to see the game; but we replayed it for them. I stood in the middle of the living room and I pretended to be Butch, and Eric stood by the piano bench, which was home plate. I threw that pitch; he hit that ball. He went around the bases and Eric slid safe under the piano bench. We all stood up and gave him a standing ovation, and that day we launched Eric into his Little League baseball career.

Eric is all grown up now. But at about the time he was

ready to graduate from high school, Eric came out to visit me. And he said, "Uncle John, I've got something exciting to tell you. You remember my first Little League baseball game?"

"Of course I do," I said, and we reminisced about it.

"I've never forgotten it," Eric said. "And I just wanted to tell you, this year I'm going to college on a baseball scholarship."

You don't have to be rich, famous, or talented to help others win. You just need to care and do your best to help them. And know this: when you have the ability to help someone win, you will be that person's friend for life.

JOHN ... WITH A MAXWELL MENTORING MOMENT

Helping another person to win is one of the greatest feelings in the world. I haven't met a person yet who doesn't like to win. And everyone I know who's made the effort to help others has said that it is the most rewarding part of life. As poet Ralph Waldo Emerson said, "It is one of the most beautiful compensations of life that no man can sincerely try to help another without helping himself."

> "It is one of the most beautiful compensations of life that no man can sincerely try to help another without helping himself."
>
> —RALPH WALDO EMERSON

If you want to help people win, then take the following steps:

BELIEVE IN PEOPLE

After a conference in Toledo, a man came up to me and asked a pointed question: "How do I get unbelievable results from a person?"

"Have unbelievable expectations about that person," was my answer.

If you don't believe in people, then you are unlikely to do everything you can to help them win. People know when someone doesn't believe in them. They see right through pretense and insincere backslapping. But when they know you believe in them, magic begins to happen. What writer John Spalding said is true: "Those who believe in our ability do more than stimulate us, they create for us an atmosphere in which it becomes easier to succeed."

GIVE PEOPLE HOPE

A reporter asked Prime Minister Winston Churchill, who led Britain during the dark moments of the Second World War, what was the greatest weapon his country possessed against the Nazi regime of Hitler. Without pausing for even a moment, Churchill said, "It was what England's greatest weapon has always been—hope."

Hope is one of the most powerful and energizing words in the English language. It is something that gives us power to keep going in the toughest of times. And its power energizes us with excitement and anticipation as we look toward the future.

It's been said that a person can live forty days without food, four days without water, four minutes without air, but only four seconds without hope. If you want to help people win, then become a purveyor of hope.

Focus on the Process, Not Just the Win

Many of us desire the win so much that we forget what it takes to get there. We're like the kid who plays chess with his grandfather. When he loses, he says, "Oh no! Not again! Grampa, you always win!"

"What do you want me to do, lose on purpose?" the old man replies. "You won't learn anything if I do that!"

"I don't wanna learn anything," the boy says. "I just wanna win!"

That's the way we often feel, but let's be honest. Which wins are the most satisfying: the easy ones or the ones we really have to work for? When you help somebody win, don't just hand it to him, even if it's in your power to do so. Help *him* win. If you assist him in the process, then you're not just giving him the victory; you're giving him the means for additional future victories. He can win and win again. And the only thing sweeter than a win is a whole bunch of wins.

Understand That When You Help Others Win, You Also Win

In 1984, Lou Whittaker led the first all-American team to the summit of Mt. Everest. After months of grueling effort, five members of the team reached the final campsite at twenty-seven thousand feet. With two thousand feet to go, they met in a crowded tent. Whittaker had a tough decision to make: he knew how highly motivated all five climbers were to stand on the highest point on earth. But two would have to go back to the previous camp, load up food, water, and oxygen, then return to the camp where they now met. After completing this support assignment, these two climbers would be in no condition to make a try for the summit. The others would stay in the tent that day to drink water, breathe oxygen, and rest, preparing them for the summit attempt the next day.

The first decision Whittaker made was to stay at the twenty-seven-thousand-foot camp to coordinate the team's activities. The next was to send the two strongest climbers down the mountain to get the supplies; it was the tougher job. The two weaker climbers would rest, renew their strength, and receive the glory of the summit.

When asked why he didn't assign himself the summit run, his answer showed his understanding of people and the strength of his leadership. He said, "My job was to put other people on top."

Whittaker understood that when people make the right decisions that help the team to achieve its goal, everybody wins. You can't help winning when you help others win.

LES ... ON BRINGING IT HOME

When I think back, I can remember many people in my life who have helped me to win. The chair of the psychology department at the college I went to honed my vision for graduate school. He showed me what steps to take and how to succeed. George, a friend of mine, helped me win by showing me how to land and host a radio show. Janice, my publicist, helps me win every time she gets me on a national television show to talk about one of my books. Kevin, another friend, helped me win by showing me how to craft a meaningful mission statement for my life. Of course, John has helped me win in my career on several fronts. Everyone likes to win. And nobody wins without help.

More than three decades ago, a research study examined the kinds of people who relate well to others. It looked at 268 Harvard sophomore men, considered to be "the best and the brightest," and followed them for forty years. Among the findings was the fact that men who were emotionally healthiest recognized that a good life was not about the absence of problems, but about how one chooses to react to problems. In other words, these men perceived themselves as winners and helped others to win in spite of their circumstances. Not surprisingly, they also had far more meaningful relationships with others.[1]

To apply John's teaching to your own life . . .

Forget about:

Approaching life as a competition where you have to beat everyone else in order to win.

Ask:

Whom would I most like to help win and how can I do it?

Do it:

Make a game plan. Chart the road you will travel together on your way to victory.

Remember:

Once you help someone win, you will have a friend for life.

A CLOSING WORD
FROM JOHN

⌗

All my life, I've believed that anyone can learn to win with people. All it takes is a belief in people and a sincere desire to help them. I hope that after reading this book, you believe that too.

We also hope that you will embrace the practices Les and I have endeavored to teach. If you have already tried some of them out, then you've probably already discovered that they really do work. If you want to learn to master all of them, then here's how I suggest you proceed: put yourself on a twelve-week program for winning with people. After starting with you, select two of the practices and do them every day for an entire week. If you do that, you will go through a process where you will . . .

1. Become conscious of how that winning way works,
2. Learn the basics of how to do it,
3. Practice it until you master it, and
4. Begin to make it a habit.

You may not feel instantly comfortable doing some of them, but there isn't a single one you can't master. And of course, keep adding other practices that you learn on your own or from others. You can never learn too many ways to win with people.

Here's to your success: may you keep winning by helping others win.

NOTES

CHAPTER 1
1. James Patterson and Peter Kim, *The Day America Told the Truth* (East Rutherford, NJ: Prentice Hall Press, 1991).

CHAPTER 2
1. Wes Smith, *Hope Meadows: Real-Life Stories of Healing and Caring from an Inspiring Community* (New York: Berkley, 2001).

CHAPTER 3
1. J. G. Nicholls, "Creativity in the person who will never produce anything original and useful: The concept of creativity as a normally distributed trait," *American Psychologist*, 27 (8) (1972), 717–27.

CHAPTER 6
1. James C. Humes, *The Wit and Wisdom of Winston Churchill* (New York: Harper Perennial, 1994), 119–20.
2. Genesis 17:5.
3. Genesis 32:28.
4. Howard Gardner, *Creating Minds: An Anatomy of Creativity Seen Through the Lives of Freud, Einstein, Picasso, Stravinsky, Eliot, Graham, and Gandhi* (New York: Basic Books, 1993).

CHAPTER 7
1. Proverbs 25:11.
2. James Kouzes and Barry Posner, *Encouraging the Heart: A Leader's Guide to Rewarding and Recognizing Others* (San Francisco: Jossey-Bass Publishers, 1999).
3. H. S. Leonard, "The many faces of character," *Consulting Psychology Journal*, 49 (4) (1997), 235–45.

CHAPTER 10
1. M. E. McCullough and C. R. Snyder, "Classical source of human strength: Revisiting an old home and building a new one." *Journal of Social and Clinical Psychology*, 19 (1) (2000), 1–10.

CHAPTER 11
    1. G. E. Vaillant, "Adaptive mental mechanisms: Their role in a positive psychology," *American Psychologist*, 55 (1) (2000), 89–98.

CHAPTER 12
    1. John 8.
    2. E. E. Werner, "Resilience in development," *Current Directions in Psychological Science*, 4 (3) (1995), 81–85.

CHAPTER 13
    1. D. A. Kramer, "Wisdom as a classical source of human strength: Conceptualization and empirical inquiry," *Journal of Social and Clinical Psychology*, 19 (1) (2000), 83–101.

CHAPTER 14
    1. R. M. Ryan and E. L. Deci, "Self-determination theory and the facilitation of intrinsic motivation, social development, and well-being," *American Psychologist*, 55 (1) (2000), 68–78.

CHAPTER 15
    1. J. W. MacDevitt, "Therapist's personal therapy and professional self-awareness," *Psychotherapy*, 24 (1987), 693–703.

CHAPTER 16
    1. Les Parrott, *Counseling and Psychotherapy*, 2nd ed. (Pacific Grove, CA: Brooks/Cole/Thomson Learning, 2003).

CHAPTER 17
    1. "Walking the Mile: A Behind-the-Scenes Documentary" (Warner Home Video, 1999).
    2. Belden Lane, "Rabbinical Stories," *Christian Century*, 98:41 (16 December 1981).
    3. Ken Sutterfield, *The Power of an Encouraging Word* (Green Forest, AR: New Leaf, 1997).
    4. J. J. Campos and K. C. Barrett, "Toward a new understanding of emotions and their development," *Emotions Cognition, and Behavior*, eds. C. Izard, J. Kagan, and R. Zajonc (New York: Cambridge University Press, 1988).

CHAPTER 19

1. D. P. McAdams, A. Diamond, E. de St. Aubin, and E. Mansfield, "Stories of commitment: The psychosocial construction of generative lives," *Journal of Personality and Social Psychology*, 72 (3) (1997), 678–94.

CHAPTER 20

1. I. K. M. Sheldon, R. M. Ryan, L. J. Rawsthorne, and B. Ilardi, "Trait self and true self: Cross-role variation in the big-five personality traits and its relations with psychological authenticity and subjective well-being," *Journal of Personality and Social Psychology*, 73 (1997), 1380–93.

CHAPTER 21

1. Source Unknown.
2. D. P. McAdams and Ed de St. Aubin (ed.), *Generativity and Adult Development: How and Why We Care for the Next Generation* (Washington, DC: APA Books, 1998).

CHAPTER 22

1. Othello, Act III, Scene 3.
2. J. D. Brown and T. A. Mankowski, "Self-esteem, mood and self-evaluation: Changes in mood and the way you see you," *Journal of Personality and Social Psychology*, 64 (1993), 421.

CHAPTER 23

1. M. E. P. Seligman and M. Csikszentmihalyi, "Positive psychology: An introduction," *American Psychologist*, 55 (1) (2000), 5–14.

CHAPTER 24

1. S. Harter, "Authenticity," C. R. Snyder and S. J. Lopez, eds., *Handbook of Positive Psychology* (New York: Oxford University Press, 2002), 382–94.

CHAPTER 25

1. Vaillant, *Adaptation to Life* (Boston: Little Brown, 1977).

ABOUT THE AUTHORS

_&_

John C. Maxwell, known as America's expert on leadership, speaks in person to hundreds of thousands of people
each year. He has communicated his principles to Fortune
500 companies, the United States Military Academy at
West Point, international marketing organizations, the
NCAA, and professional sports groups such as the NFL.
Maxwell is the founder of several leadership organizations
dedicated to helping people reach their personal and leadership potential, such as Injoy Stewardship Services. He
dedicates much of his time to training leaders worldwide
through EQUIP, a non-profit organization. A _New York
Times_ bestselling author with more than 8 million books in
print, Dr. Maxwell has written more than thirty books,
including _Developing the Leader Within You, Today Matters,_
and _The 21 Irrefutable Laws of Leadership,_ which has sold
more than one million copies.

Les Parrott, Ph.D., is founder of the Center for
Relationship Development on the campus of Seattle Pacific
University and the best-selling author of _High-Maintenance
Relationships, The Control Freak, Shoulda Coulda Woulda,_
and _Love Talk._ Dr. Parrott is a sought after speaker to
Fortune 500 companies and holds relationship seminars
across North America. He communicates annually to a

wide variety of audiences, including professional athletes, government agencies, military personnel, and business leaders. He also hosts the national radio broadcast "Love Talk." Dr Parrott has been featured in *USA Today*, the *Wall Street Journal*, and the *New York Times*. His television appearances include *The View*, *The O'Reilly Factor*, CNN, *Good Morning America*, and *Oprah*.

To learn about his speaking availability and seminar schedules, as well as all of Dr. Parrott's resources, contact: www.RealRelationships.com.

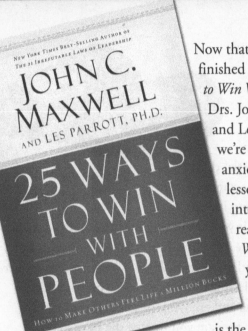

Step 1: Reinforce Your Foundation

Winning with people isn't a natural gift; it's a nurtured one. That's why it is so important to continually expose your mind to material that reinforces the importance of relationship building in *your*

Relationships — The First Step to Success

life. When you visit **www.WinningWithPeopleBook.com**, you will receive access to a free lesson on relationships by John Maxwell entitled, *Relationships — The First Step to Success*. This entertaining lesson contains valuable information on building, nurturing and enjoying successful relationships and will effectively prepare you to take the next step in relationship construction.

Relationships — The First Step to Success is available to you free of charge in streaming audio format online or on CD (for a minimal shipping charge of $2.00).

Step 1: Reinforce Your Foundation

If you haven't read *Winning With People* yet, we highly recommend this wonderful resource. *Winning With People* provides you with the tools you need to immediately improve your existing relationships as well as cultivate strong, exciting, and new ones. Using a unique blend of interesting facts, statistics, humor, real-life examples, and questions for discussion, *Winning With People* reveals the key people principles for true success in life. Order your own copy of *Winning With People* today at www.WinningWithPeopleBook.com.

Step 2: Prepare Your Foundation for Construction

Step two provides the framework that will house and shelter your relationships. Based on John Maxwell's best-selling book, *Winning With People,* the *Winning With People DVD Training Curriculum* takes an in-depth look at his 25

People Principles. This training curriculum is designed both for individual and team study. You and your team will learn practices that make significant changes in the relationships of those you interact with from inside the team and beyond.

Through this course, you will:

- **Improve** your relationship skills and those of your team
- **Enhance** your team's communication and teamwork skills
- **Understand** how strong, healthy, and effective relationships can breed long-term success
- **Experience** stronger and higher quality interactions with those around you
- **Learn** how to work with various types of personalities to achieve common goals

Step 3: Build Your Leadership Development Program

Now that you have built up your ability to create and manage strong, healthy relationships, it's time to ramp up your leadership training curriculum. To facilitate your leadership skills training, Maximum Impact has two monthly audio programs — **The Maximum Impact Club** and the **Leadership Today Audio Series**. With these programs you will learn from some of the greatest leadership minds of our day: **John C. Maxwell, Pat Williams, Mark Sanborn, Pat Summitt**, and many more. Make a significant difference in your life today by joining one of these stellar programs. You will be amazed at the results and excited about awakening the potential within you!

The Maximum Impact Monthly Mentoring Club brings John C. Maxwell to you each and every month. Turn your drive time into a "leadership university" by subscribing to this powerful monthly resource. John will present relevant, insightful content to you each month in a CD or audiocassette format.

Step 3: Build Your Leadership Development Program

Leadership Today gives you the opportunity to hear about the successes and trials of

modern day leaders and how they have transformed challenges into accomplishments. Past lessons have included insights from these accomplished leaders: **Tim Sanders,** Leadership Coach at Yahoo and author of the popular book *Love is the Killer App;* **Brigadier General Leo A. Brooks, Jr.,** The 68th Commandant of the United States Corps of Cadets at West Point; and **Michael Duke,** President and Chief Executive Officer of the Wal-Mart Stores, USA.

No matter what level of success you have achieved, you can always learn from others. The **Leadership Today** Audio Program continues to bring leaders to you each and every month. Available on CD, listen to these powerful lessons on your way to work or at the computer.

Visit us at www.WinningWithPeopleBook.com
to begin the leadership journey of a lifetime!

Step 4: Furnish Your Relationship and Leadership Home

Step four introduces you to the most powerful leadership training that Maximum Impact currently offers. **Maximum Impact's Corporate Training** takes John C. Maxwell's principles to the next level using workshops in leadership, teamwork, and personal development.

Values-based Leadership Development

The Developing the Leader Within You™ two-day workshop is a values-based, facilitator-lead interactive experience that allows you to raise your level of influence. This course takes content from John's best-selling books *The 21 Irrefutable Laws of Leadership, Developing the Leader Within You,* and *Developing the Leader Around You* and allows you to see who you really are in terms of your personal leadership behaviors and chart a course that will yield outstanding results.

Teamwork

In addition to leadership development training, you can build your business or organization with our **Teamwork Training Workshops.** These highly interactive and fun experiences explore the dynamics of great teams and teach these principles with tactile and textbook instruction. These workshops are available by appointment and are held at your location or at

To learn more about Maximum Impact Corporate Training workshops, visit www.WinningWithPeopleBook.com today!

Step 4: Furnish Your Relationship and Leadership Home

your planned retreat or conference. We illustrate John Maxwell's teambuilding principles and bring them to life for you to bring to your team. Based on John's books *The 17 indisputable Laws of Teamwork* and *The 17 Qualities of a Team Player,* these dynamic workshops put a framework in place that you can replicate with confidence at your organization.

Leadership and Teamwork PowerShops
Does your organization have a meeting event, conference, or management retreat that needs to introduce or reinforce leadership or teambuilding principles? A **Maximum Impact PowerShop** may be the perfect solution. Whether a breakout session, a keynote, or class, a **Leadership PowerShop** or a **Teamwork PowerShop** takes John Maxwell's principles and abbreviates and tailors the message for your audience. The PowerShop is hands-on teaching that sticks in the minds of the participants. This training ranges in scope and duration based on your event's needs. Perfect for introducing a new leadership or teambuilding initiative, the PowerShop will bring a high-energy and tangible experience to your group.

Get the resources necessary to build stronger relationships and to create new exciting relationships at www.WinningWithPeopleBook.com.